BRAIN GAMES®

USELESS TRIVIA PUZZLES

pil

Publications International, Ltd.

Puzzle creators: Holli Fort, Christopher Lagerstrom, Jill Oldham, and Marty Strasen

Images from Shutterstock.com

Brain Games is a registered trademark of Publications International, Ltd.

Louis Weber, CEO
Publications International, Ltd.
8140 Lehigh Avenue
Morton Grove, IL 60053

ISBN: 978-1-64030-094-1

Manufactured in China.

8 7 6 5 4 3 2 1

TABLE OF CONTENTS

HOW TO PLAY

Welcome to *Useless Trivia Puzzles.* This is not your typical trivia book. If you're looking for dry and dusty trivia, you won't find it here. But if you think you know—or want to know—what European capital has more dogs than people, who authored the first novel written on a typewriter, which former Beatle was the first person to be featured on the cover of *Rolling Stone,* or what the Scoville scale measures, you've come to the right place. Here you'll discover where the world's deepest lake is located, what substance ancient Romans used as a tooth whitener, the average life expectancy for a one-dollar bill, and many other useless trivia facts.

Each chapter has a theme, making it easy for you to pick your favorite category. If you're a geography bee champ, start with chapter 1. If music is your thing, head to chapter 8. If you think you know how many spikes there are in the Statue of Liberty's crown, check out Americana. You'll find questions on the right-hand pages and answers on the following pages, along with a few extra tidbits of information.

Are you ready to put your trivia know-how to the test? Grab a pencil, pull out *Useless Trivia Puzzles,* and get ready for an entertaining time!

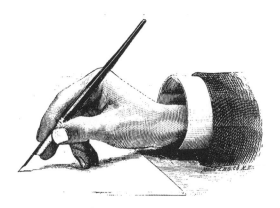

GEOGRAPHY

1. What is the biggest city (by population) in North America?

- [ ] A. Toronto
- [ ] B. New York City
- [ ] C. Mexico City
- [ ] D. Los Angeles

- [ ] A. Saint Helena
- [ ] B. Bouvet Island
- [ ] C. Easter Island
- [ ] D. Kiribati

2. *What is the most remote island in the world?*

3. What European capital is home to more dogs than people?

- [ ] A. London
- [ ] B. Berlin
- [ ] C. Paris
- [ ] D. Amsterdam

ANSWERS

1. **C.** With a population of 8.9 million, Mexico City beats out all the competition.

In 2013, Toronto (population 2.79 million) overtook Chicago to become the fourth-largest city in North America.

2. **B.** *This South Atlantic island is almost a thousand miles away from its closest neighbor, Queen Maude Land, Antarctica. If you need to borrow a cup of sugar, though, you're out of luck— the island is uninhabited.*

3. **C.** When visiting the French capital, attention *à la marche* (watch your step).

QUESTIONS

4. Where is the world's largest ice skating area?

☐ **A. Ottawa, Ontario, Canada**
☐ **B. Vaasa, Finland**
☐ **C. Moscow, Russia**
☐ **D. Nuuk, Greenland**

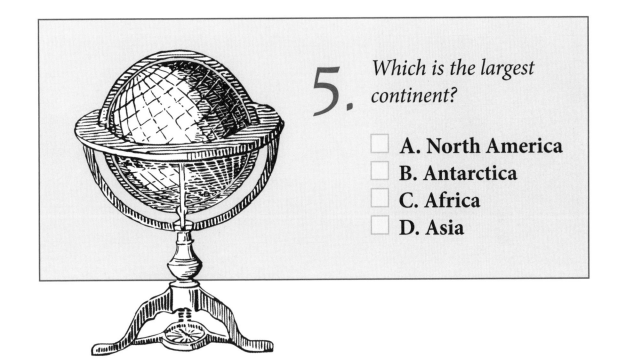

5. *Which is the largest continent?*

☐ **A. North America**
☐ **B. Antarctica**
☐ **C. Africa**
☐ **D. Asia**

6. What is the collective name for the vast rural areas of Australia?

☐ **A. Great Plains**
☐ **B. Big Steppes**
☐ **C. Outback**
☐ **D. Centrelands**

ANSWERS

4. **A.** *If you've got the time and the stamina, you can skate 4.8 miles on Ottawa's Rideau Canal Skateway.*

5. **D.** Asia is the largest continent both by land mass (44,579,000 square miles) and population (4.4 billion).

6. **C.** It's not just a great steakhouse! The Outback is also nicknamed "the back of beyond" and "beyond the black stump."

QUESTIONS

7. What is the capital of Turkey?

- ☐ A. Ankara
- ☐ B. Istanbul
- ☐ C. Bursa
- ☐ D. Adana

8. The deepest area in the world's oceans shares a name with which space shuttle?

- ☐ A. *Atlantis*
- ☐ B. *Challenger*
- ☐ C. *Columbia*
- ☐ D. *Discovery*

- ☐ A. Brazil
- ☐ B. Colombia
- ☐ C. Bolivia
- ☐ D. Peru

9. *Which South American country is home to the ancient city of Machu Picchu?*

ANSWERS

7. **A.** This planned city beat out its big sister Istanbul because of its position right in the center of the country—much to the Turkish delight of its residents!

8. **B.** *Challenger Deep is named after the ship whose crew discovered the depth—nearly seven miles!—of this part of the Pacific Ocean.*

9. **D.** The ancient home of the Inca Empire used to be a six-day walk from civilization, but now train travelers can leave from Cusco and get there in mere hours.

Even without mortar, the stones that make up the citadel of Machu Picchu fit together so tightly that even a knife blade won't fit in the seams.

QUESTIONS

10. Amsterdam is sometimes called the "Venice of the North." How many canals does it have?

- ☐ **A. 55**
- ☐ **B. 105**
- ☐ **C. 165**
- ☐ **D. 215**

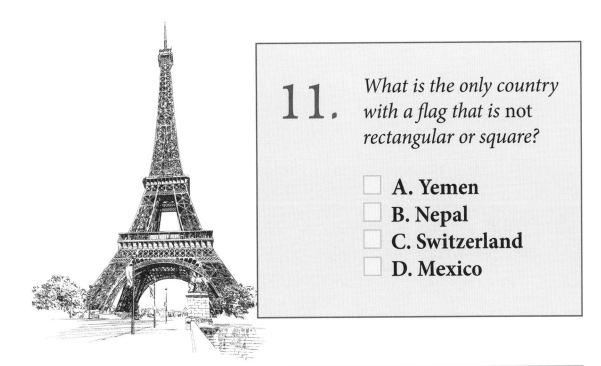

11. *What is the only country with a flag that is not rectangular or square?*

- ☐ **A. Yemen**
- ☐ **B. Nepal**
- ☐ **C. Switzerland**
- ☐ **D. Mexico**

- ☐ **A. Big Ben**
- ☐ **B. Leaning Tower of Pisa**
- ☐ **C. Eiffel Tower**
- ☐ **D. Giralda Tower**

12. Which landmark shrinks about six inches every winter?

ANSWERS

10. **C.** And along with the canals are 1,281 bridges, most of which open to let ships pass through and provide Dutch schoolchildren with a handy "The bridge was open" excuse for tardiness. Hey, it beats "The dog ate my homework."

11. **B.** Nepal's flag is made of two joined triangular shapes with sun and moon designs.

Switzerland and Vatican City are the only countries with square flags.

12. **C.** *Like a swimmer in cold water, the metal tower is susceptible to temperature-induced shrinkage.*

QUESTIONS

13. Where is the Colosseum located?

☐ **A. Athens**
☐ **B. Florence**
☐ **C. Jerusalem**
☐ **D. Rome**

☐ **A. Barcelona**
☐ **B. Madrid**
☐ **C. Pamplona**
☐ **D. Valencia**

14. In what Spanish city does the famous "running of the bulls" festival take place each July?

15. *Take a trip to Easter Island and you'll find yourself vacationing with which magnificent statues?*

☐ **A. 4,012 Golems**
☐ **B. 887 Moai**
☐ **C. 263 Koias**
☐ **D. 8,045 Sirhc**

ANSWERS

13. **D.** *The arena was built in A.D. 80 and was primarily a venue where Romans enjoyed gladiator battles and wild animal fights.*

14.

C. Olé! Unlike bullfights, which are open only to professionals, anyone age 18 or older is welcome to participate in the *encierro* (running of the bulls).

15. **B.** Easter Island, a Polynesian island in the Pacific Ocean, is home to 887 statues known as Moai. They were created by the Rapa Nui people and are found mostly near the coasts of Rapa Nui, the Polynesian name for the island. Easter Island can rightfully be called the middle of nowhere; the closest inhabited island is more than 1,200 miles away, and that island only has 50 permanent residents.

QUESTIONS

16. Lake Baikal, the deepest lake on Earth, is located within which continent?

- A. Asia
- B. Europe
- C. Africa
- D. Australia

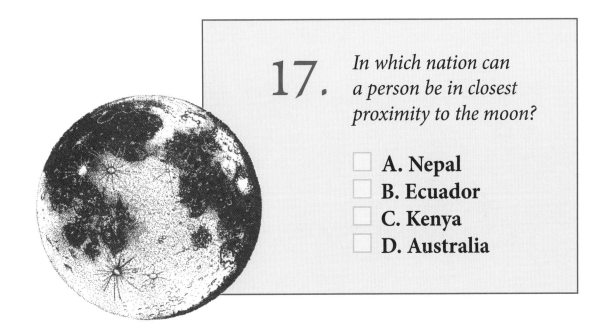

17. *In which nation can a person be in closest proximity to the moon?*

- A. Nepal
- B. Ecuador
- C. Kenya
- D. Australia

- A. Glassblowing
- B. Metal forging
- C. Pottery
- D. Wineries

18. The island of Murano is located off the coast of Venice, Italy. For what is it best known?

ANSWERS

16. **A.** Cold, cold, COLD Lake Baikal is found in Siberia, with basins in both Russia and Mongolia. It's not only the deepest lake on the planetZ, but also Earth's clearest and most voluminous freshwater lake, accounting for more than 20 percent of the world's unfrozen surface freshwater. And it's thought to be the world's oldest lake, having been around for approximately 25 million years.

17. **B.** Most people think of Earth as a perfectly round sphere. Actually, it's shaped more like a beach ball squeezed at both ends—an oblate spheroid, to get technical. According to scientists, you'd be a mile-and-a-half closer to outer space if you stood atop Ecuador's Chimborazo volcano than you would be standing at the summit of Mount Everest, on the border between China and Nepal. Everest climbs highest in terms of sea level; Chimborazo's highest point is farther from the Earth's core.

A. *The island's reputation as a center for artisan glass dates back to the 13th century.* **18.**

QUESTIONS

19. What's the only city in the world that's located on two continents?

☐ **A. Cairo, Egypt**
☐ **B. Anchorage, Alaska, U.S.A.**
☐ **C. Ceuta, Spain**
☐ **D. Istanbul, Turkey**

20. What is the official language of Brazil?

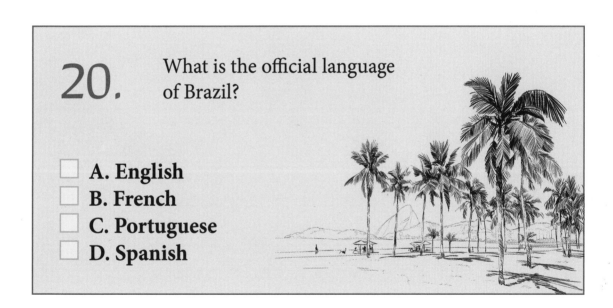

☐ **A. English**
☐ **B. French**
☐ **C. Portuguese**
☐ **D. Spanish**

☐ **A. England**
☐ **B. Ireland**
☐ **C. Scotland**
☐ **D. Wales**

21. *Where is Stonehenge?*

ANSWERS

19. **D.** Istanbul, Turkey. Istanbul flanks the Bosporus Strait between Asia and Europe. (See, all those years of studying for the National Geographic Geography Bee finally paid off!)

20. **C.** Brazil is the only nation in South America whose official language is Portuguese. Most of the other South American countries claim Spanish as their national language, although French (French Guiana), English (Guyana), and Dutch (Suriname) also make the list.

21. **A.** Okay, we know *where* the prehistoric monument is (Wiltshire County, southwest England), but do we know *what* it is? Not really. The best guesses include a temple for sun worship, a healing center, a burial site, and a huge calendar.

QUESTIONS

22. Which river flows through the Grand Canyon?

- ☐ **A. Colorado**
- ☐ **B. Columbia**
- ☐ **C. Green**
- ☐ **D. Rio Grande**

23. In what country is the world's tallest building?

- ☐ **A. Malaysia**
- ☐ **B. Qatar**
- ☐ **C. China**
- ☐ **D. United Arab Emirates**

- ☐ **A. Amazon**
- ☐ **B. Mississippi**
- ☐ **C. Nile**
- ☐ **D. Yangtze**

24. *What is the longest river in the world?*

ANSWERS

22. **A.** *The Colorado River is the Southwest's longest river. It begins in the Rocky Mountains in Colorado and flows almost 1,500 miles before emptying into the Gulf of California in Mexico.*

23. **D.** At 2,722.57 feet, the Burj Khalifa in Dubai, UAE, is the tallest man-made structure in the world. It was completed in 2010.

The Burj Khalifa may soon relinquish its title. If completed in 2020 as planned, the Jeddah Tower in Saudi Arabia will surpass the Burj Khalifa.

24. **C.** At 4,132 miles long, the Nile, which starts in Lake Victoria and flows north through Africa all the way to the Mediterranean Sea, is more than 100 miles longer than its closest competitor (the Amazon, in South America).

THE HUMAN BODY

1. What is the name of the bone that extends from the shoulder to the elbow?

☐ **A. Humerus**
☐ **B. Lunate**
☐ **C. Radius**
☐ **D. Ulna**

☐ **A. Lung**
☐ **B. Kidney**
☐ **C. Heart**
☐ **D. Liver**

2. *What was the first human organ to be successfully transplanted?*

3. Which item is responsible for most cases of choking in the United States?

☐ **A. Pen/pencil**
☐ **B. Toothpick**
☐ **C. Peanut**
☐ **D. Carrot**

ANSWERS

1. **A.** The humerus is also known as the funny bone, and that's no joke. That last sentence was a joke, though. Did it tickle your humerus? (Not to be confused with humor, which is the fluid that fills your eyeballs.)

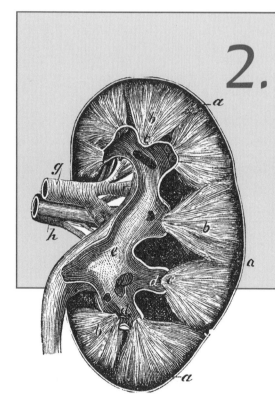

2. **B.** *The first successful transplant took place in 1954 in Boston. Since the surgery predated the discovery of anti-rejection drugs, it was a good thing the patients were identical twins so the organ was not rejected.*

3. **B.** Maybe stick to floss next time…

QUESTIONS

4. What part of your body would you use for gurning?

- ☐ **A. Hands**
- ☐ **B. Abs**
- ☐ **C. Face**
- ☐ **D. Shoulders**

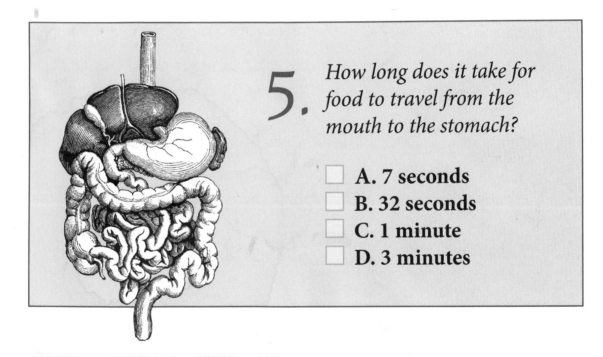

5. *How long does it take for food to travel from the mouth to the stomach?*

- ☐ **A. 7 seconds**
- ☐ **B. 32 seconds**
- ☐ **C. 1 minute**
- ☐ **D. 3 minutes**

6. A laugh expels air out of the body at speeds up to 70 miles per hour. What is the speed of the air released with a sneeze?

- ☐ **A. 80 miles per hour**
- ☐ **B. 100 miles per hour**
- ☐ **C. 120 miles per hour**
- ☐ **D. 140 miles per hour**

ANSWERS

4. **C.** Gurning is a contest in which professionals compete to see who can pull the "world's ugliest face." Those who practice enough might make it to the Egremont Gurning Championship, held every September in Cumbria, England.

5. **B.** *And it doesn't take much longer from the lips to the hips!*

6. **B.** The sneeze is a powerful weapon—it can send 100,000 germs into the air in a single speedy bound!

Ever sneezed in your sleep? Most people don't because the nerve that causes sneezing goes to sleep when you do.

QUESTIONS

7. If you accidentally knock out a tooth, in what liquid should you store it to improve the chances of the dentist being able to re-implant it?

- ☐ **A. Beer (preferably stout)**
- ☐ **B. Water**
- ☐ **C. Juice**
- ☐ **D. Milk**

8. Everyone knows not to leave fingerprints behind if they want to keep their identity unrevealed. What other body part has a unique print?

- ☐ **A. Nose**
- ☐ **B. Tongue**
- ☐ **C. Ear**
- ☐ **D. Elbow**

- ☐ **A. 182**
- ☐ **B. 206**
- ☐ **C. 274**
- ☐ **D. 302**

9. *We begin our lives with more than 300 bones, but some of those 300 fuse together during growth. How many bones do adults have?*

ANSWERS

7. **D.** The proteins and antibacterial properties of milk keep the cells alive—definitely doing the body good.

8. **B.** *Yet another reason not to lick doorknobs.*

9. **C.** Good thing bones don't continue to fuse—we wouldn't be much more flexible than Barbie and Ken dolls.

QUESTIONS

10. What is the most common blood type?

- ☐ A. B+
- ☐ B. O-
- ☐ C. AB
- ☐ D. O+

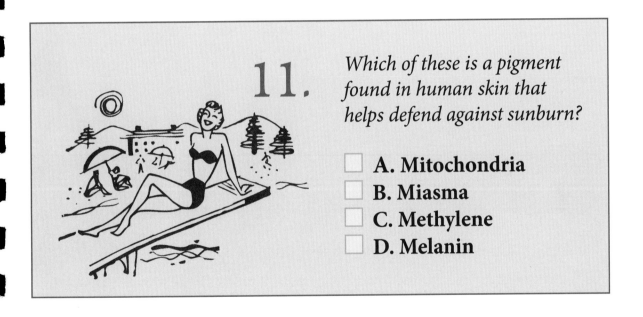

11. *Which of these is a pigment found in human skin that helps defend against sunburn?*

- ☐ **A. Mitochondria**
- ☐ **B. Miasma**
- ☐ **C. Methylene**
- ☐ **D. Melanin**

- ☐ **A. Vermiform appendix**
- ☐ **B. Wisdom teeth**
- ☐ **C. Auriclares muscles**
- ☐ **D. Semilunar folds**

12. Which of the following body parts is no longer required by humans?

ANSWERS

10. **D.** However, the O- blood type is the universal donor, meaning all other blood types can mix with it. That's why TV and movie doctors so often call for "O Neg." But people who have O- blood can only receive O- blood, and they make up less than 8% of the total U.S. population. To get an A+ on this blood test, you should also know that AB- is the rarest blood type—less than 1% of the total U.S. population has it.

11. **D.** Melanin is found in most living organisms, but one major exception is spiders. With or without melanin, spiders make some people's skin crawl!

12. **All of the above.** *The vermiform appendix was probably been your first guess, but wisdom teeth (leftovers from the era in which people chewed more foliage), auriclares muscles (those that redirect your ears), and semilunar folds (the fold in the corner of the eye, a vestigial remnant of another eyelid) are all nonessential in modern humans. Of course, only the appendix has been known to explode.*

QUESTIONS

13. What is the colored part of the eye called?

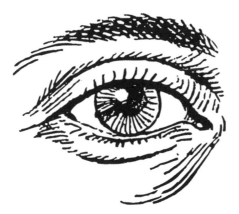

☐ **A. Cornea**
☐ **B. Iris**
☐ **C. Pupil**
☐ **D. Retina**

☐ **A. Calcium**
☐ **B. Magnesium**
☐ **C. Vitamin A**
☐ **D. Vitamin D**

14. What nutrient do we absorb from exposure to sunlight?

15. *In 1955, Jonas Salk discovered a vaccine for what disease?*

☐ **A. Polio**
☐ **B. Measles**
☐ **C. Mumps**
☐ **D. Rubella**

ANSWERS

13. **B.** *The most common eye color in the world is brown. The least common is green. So what's the bestselling colored contact lens, you wonder? There's no record of that, but it's probably not cat's eyes.*

14. **D.** Hence vitamin D's nickname: the sunshine vitamin. If you're looking to amp up your vitamin D intake, turn to mushrooms, fatty fish, beef liver, or eggs. Intake means you're supposed to eat them—not bask in their glow.

15. **A.** Incredibly, Salk chose not to patent the vaccine. On his decision, Salk said: "There is no patent. Could you patent the sun?" Who holds the patent on selfless scientists?

QUESTIONS

16. Which organ produces insulin?

- ☐ A. Kidney
- ☐ B. Liver
- ☐ C. Pancreas
- ☐ D. Small intestine

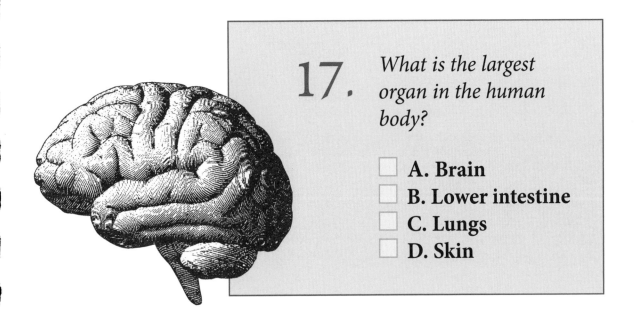

17. *What is the largest organ in the human body?*

- ☐ A. Brain
- ☐ B. Lower intestine
- ☐ C. Lungs
- ☐ D. Skin

- ☐ A. Excessive blinking
- ☐ B. Goose bumps
- ☐ C. Impotence
- ☐ D. Vomiting

18. What symptom does *piloerection* cause?

ANSWERS

16. **C.** Insulin is a hormone that moves sugar out of the blood and into the body's cells. You can think of it as a key that unlocks the door to the cell so that food (sugar/glucose) can get inside and feed it. A deficiency of insulin can lead to diabetes.

D. *The average person sheds nearly 1.5 pounds of skin per year. After 50 years, you'll have left 75 pounds of old skin lying around! Try and shed that image.* **17.**

18. **B.** *Piloerection* isn't as naughty as it sounds. It's an involuntary reflex that causes the muscles around the base of each hair follicle to contract, making the hairs stand up and causing small bumps to appear. They're referred to as goose bumps because a cold or frightened person's reactive skin resembles a plucked goose's hide. Lovely.

QUESTIONS

19. Which of the following facts about crying is *not* true?

☐ A. Tears release toxins that reduce stress
☐ B. The scent of women's tears reduces men's sexual arousal
☐ C. You can't cry with your eyes closed
☐ D. There are three types of tears

20. Which famous actor is a great example of heterochromia?

☐ A. Tom Cruise
☐ B. Julia Roberts
☐ C. Tom Hanks
☐ D. Jane Seymour

☐ A. Obstetrics
☐ B. Cardiology
☐ C. Orthopedics
☐ D. Urology

21. *In which field of medicine is amniocentesis used?*

ANSWERS

19. **C.** You practically can't sneeze with your eyes open, or effectively yawn (which cools down the brain, scientists say), but you can certainly cry with your eyes shut. And in case you're wondering, the three types of tears aren't crocodile, happy, and "of a clown." The real types are basal (lubricant), reflexive (when injured), and psych (emotional).

20. **D.** Seymour has eyes that are two different colors: one is brown and the other is green. Mila Kunis, Dan Ackroyd, and Kate Bosworth also have heterochromia.

D. *This test screens for potential problems with a fetus— and can tell gender.* **21.**

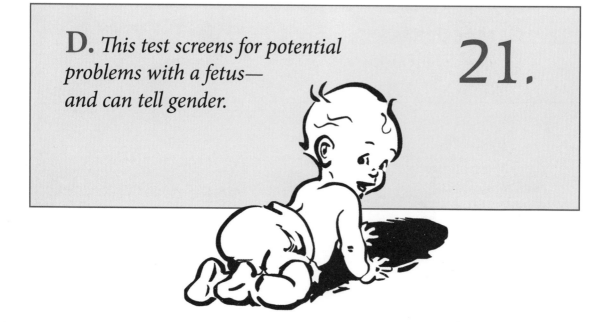

QUESTIONS

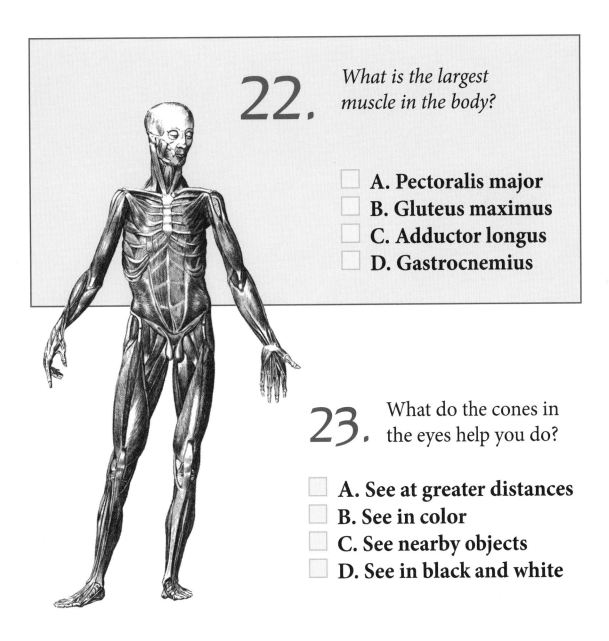

22. *What is the largest muscle in the body?*

☐ **A. Pectoralis major**
☐ **B. Gluteus maximus**
☐ **C. Adductor longus**
☐ **D. Gastrocnemius**

23. What do the cones in the eyes help you do?

☐ **A. See at greater distances**
☐ **B. See in color**
☐ **C. See nearby objects**
☐ **D. See in black and white**

ANSWERS

B. All that junk is there to support your trunk.

22.

23. **B.** *Each eye has 6 to 7 million cones to help you find just the right shade of blue.*

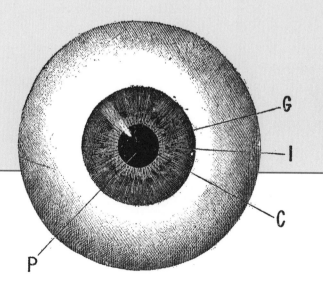

FOOD AND DRINK

1. Which of the following was *not* one of the General Mills monster cereals?

- [ ] A. Fruit Brute
- [ ] B. Boo Berry
- [ ] C. Zombie Puffs
- [ ] D. Yummy Mummy

- [ ] A. Turkey & Gravy
- [ ] B. Salmon Paté
- [ ] C. Antacid
- [ ] D. Roasted Garlic Hummus

2. *Which of the following was* not *a limited-edition flavor of Jones Soda?*

3. Until the nineteenth century, most Americans believed that the "love apple" (tomato) was what?

- [ ] A. A vegetable
- [ ] B. Poisonous
- [ ] C. The original apple from the Garden of Eden
- [ ] D. A natural antacid

ANSWERS

1. C. And it's too bad, because Zombie Puffs would have fit right in with Count Chocula, Franken Berry, and the rest of the gang.

2. D. We'd rather drink that than the Seahawks Collector Pack flavors Perspiration, Natural Field Turf, and Dirt . . . but just barely.

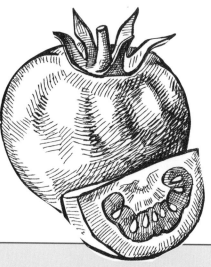

3. B. *To prove that tomatoes were perfectly safe, in 1820, Robert Gibbon stood on the courthouse steps in Salem, New Jersey, and ate an entire basket of tomatoes in front of the townspeople. No word on what he did to treat the heartburn that no doubt followed this exercise.*

QUESTIONS

4. Contrary to popular belief, the tomato is a fruit, not a vegetable. Which of these other plants is *not* a vegetable?

- [ ] **A. Cucumber**
- [ ] **B. Broccoli**
- [ ] **C. Asparagus**
- [ ] **D. Turnip**

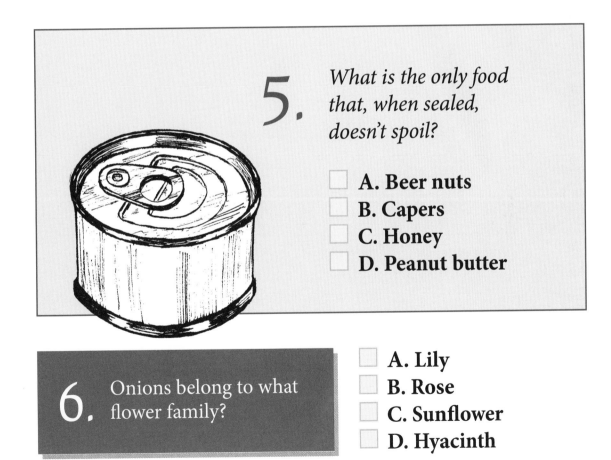

5. *What is the only food that, when sealed, doesn't spoil?*

- [ ] **A. Beer nuts**
- [ ] **B. Capers**
- [ ] **C. Honey**
- [ ] **D. Peanut butter**

6. Onions belong to what flower family?

- [ ] **A. Lily**
- [ ] **B. Rose**
- [ ] **C. Sunflower**
- [ ] **D. Hyacinth**

ANSWERS

4. **A.** Cucumbers are scientifically classified as fruits. They belong to the same plant family as watermelons, pumpkins, zucchini, and squash.

5. **C.** *Airtight containers will make honey last forever—literally! Several giant vats of honey, untouched for more than 3,000 years, were excavated from King Tut's tomb. Incredibly, the honey was found to still be edible.*

A. Also in this very pungent family: garlic, leeks, and chives. **6.**

"An onion can make people cry but there's never been a vegetable that can make people laugh."
—*Will Rogers*

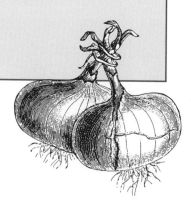

QUESTIONS

7. If you went to a diner and ordered a "Burn the British," what would you get?

- ☐ **A. Hard-boiled eggs**
- ☐ **B. Toasted English muffins**
- ☐ **C. French toast**
- ☐ **D. Short stack of pancakes**

8. Which of these is *not* an actual week dedicated to an offbeat food?

- ☐ **A. Solo Diners Eat Out Week**
- ☐ **B. Eat Dessert First Week**
- ☐ **C. Stuff Yourself Silly Week**
- ☐ **D. Gluten-Free Baking Week**

- ☐ **A. John Malkovich**
- ☐ **B. Bela Lugosi**
- ☐ **C. Willem Dafoe**
- ☐ **D. Vincent Price**

9. *Which creepy actor also penned a gourmet cookbook?*

ANSWERS

7. **B.** *And if you're in the mood for butter, you could order it "with cow to cover."*

8. **C.** To be fair, though, there is an Eat What You Want Day (May 11). Everything in moderation, just like we always say.

9. **D.** Long before he did the voiceover for Michael Jackson's *Thriller*, Price and his wife, Mary, penned the terrifyingly good *A Treasury of Great Recipes* (1965).

QUESTIONS

10. Refreshing lemon-lime soda 7-Up originally counted which substance among its ingredients?

- ☐ **A. Cocaine**
- ☐ **B. Lithium**
- ☐ **C. Valium**
- ☐ **D. Heroin**

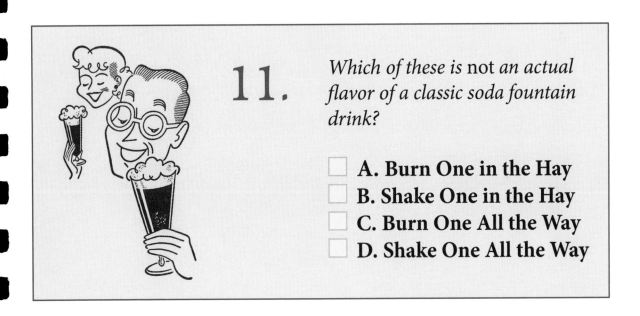

11. *Which of these is not an actual flavor of a classic soda fountain drink?*

- ☐ **A. Burn One in the Hay**
- ☐ **B. Shake One in the Hay**
- ☐ **C. Burn One All the Way**
- ☐ **D. Shake One All the Way**

- ☐ **A. The fattiness of a cut of meat**
- ☐ **B. The purity of olive oil**
- ☐ **C. The "heat" of chilies**
- ☐ **D. The clarity of wine**

12. What does the Scoville scale measure?

ANSWERS

B. *"It's an UP thing,"* indeed.   **10.**

11. **A.** Burn One All the Way is a chocolate malted; Shake One in the Hay is a strawberry milkshake; and Shake One All the Way is a chocolate milkshake.

If you asked a soda jerk to "Twist it, choke it, and make it cackle," you wanted a malted milkshake with a raw egg.

12. **C.** Are you feeling hot, hot, hot? The Scoville scale can either confirm or refute your hotness.

QUESTIONS

13. Which famous product was originally marketed as "Esteemed Brain Tonic and Intellectual Beverage"?

☐ **A. Coca-Cola**
☐ **B. Ginger Ale**
☐ **C. Maxwell House Coffee**
☐ **D. Smart Water**

☐ **A. Mushrooms**
☐ **B. Pasta**
☐ **C. Pears**
☐ **D. Snails**

14. Clamshell, table, black trumpet, and golden needle are all types of what?

15. *Natural vanilla flavoring comes from which flower?*

☐ **A. Calla lilies**
☐ **B. Dahlias**
☐ **C. Orchids**
☐ **D. Sweet peas**

ANSWERS

13. **A.** *Coca-Cola was invented in Atlanta, Georgia, where it debuted in 1886 and sold for five cents a glass.*

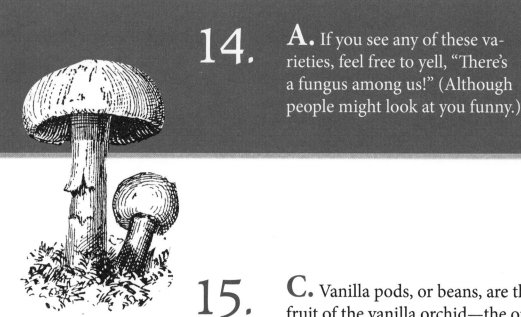

14. **A.** If you see any of these varieties, feel free to yell, "There's a fungus among us!" (Although people might look at you funny.)

15. **C.** Vanilla pods, or beans, are the fruit of the vanilla orchid—the only orchid plant that produces an edible fruit. Now, if only chocolate grew on trees... Wait a minute—it does! Cacao pods, which are used to make chocolate, grow on small tropical trees called Theobroma cacao trees.

QUESTIONS

16. At a price of more than $300 per pound, kopi luwak is the world's most expensive coffee. What makes these coffee beans so special?

- ☐ **A. Each bean is hand-roasted over an open flame**
- ☐ **B. Beans are only picked on the night of a blue moon**
- ☐ **C. Beans are picked out of animal droppings**
- ☐ **D. There are only five acres of fields in the world suited to grow these beans**

---

17. *Although milk is the state's official drink, sometimes Nebraskans have a taste for something a little less natural, so they indulge in the state's official state soft drink. What is it?*

- ☐ **A. Kool-Aid**
- ☐ **B. Pepsi**
- ☐ **C. Country Time Lemonade**
- ☐ **D. Dr. Pepper**

- ☐ **A. One-tenth of a calorie**
- ☐ **B. Three-fourths of a calorie**
- ☐ **C. Two calories**
- ☐ **D. Five calories**

18. How many calories does the adhesive on a lickable U.S. postage stamp contain?

ANSWERS

16. **C.** Civet cats eat the coffee cherries but can't digest the beans, so they pass through the animal's digestive tract and then are, um, handpicked and readied for roasting.

17. **A.** *No word on whether Kool-Aid Man had to bust through the walls at the state capital to make it happen, but Kool-Aid was designated the official soft drink in 1998.*

18. **A.** That little baby is a dietary bargain at only one-tenth of a calorie.

Cockroaches like eating the adhesive on stamps—a ringing endorsement for buying the self-stick kind.

QUESTIONS

19. Twist-ties (and plastic tabs) on bread sold in stores are color-coded. Why?

- ☐ **A. To tell which worker packaged the bread**
- ☐ **B. To tell the date the bread was baked**
- ☐ **C. To confuse consumers**
- ☐ **D. To identify the bakery where the bread was baked**

20. Horse nettle, an ingredient sometimes found in tea, boasts which of the following benefits?

- ☐ **A. Acne combatant**
- ☐ **B. Laxative**
- ☐ **C. Pick-me-up**
- ☐ **D. Sedative**

21. *Which of these sweet treats has not been featured as a main ingredient in a breakfast cereal?*

- ☐ **A. AirHeads**
- ☐ **B. Ice cream**
- ☐ **C. Raisinets**
- ☐ **D. Willy Wonka's Nerds candy**

ANSWERS

19. **B.** Much to the gratitude of stock clerks everywhere, it's much easier to pick out all the twist ties of a certain color than to squint at the tiny sell-by dates on the packages when it comes time to take old bread off the shelf.

20. **D.** Horse nettle actually has nothing to do with horses, so PETA members have nothing to worry about. You might, though—horse nettle is a flowering weed whose unripe fruit is poisonous. The ripe fruit is not harmful, however, and when cooked it has mild sedative powers. Don't try this at home, kids!

C. *Although sugar-happy tykes everywhere might think Raisin Bran could be improved by coating the raisins with chocolate, no such cereal has been created . . . yet. Cap'n Crunch's AirHeads Berries was produced by Quaker in 2003. In 1965 Kellogg's introduced Kream Krunch, which was filled with bits of freeze-dried ice cream. And the tangy flavor of Nerds candy was recreated in Nerds Cereal in the mid-1980s, with Ralston cleverly dividing the cereal box in half to feature a different flavor in each compartment, just like the candy box.* **21.**

ARTS AND LITERATURE

1. Which well-known writer coined the word "nerd"?

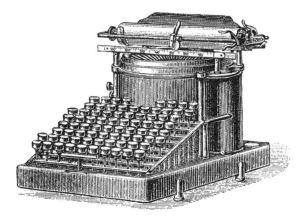

☐ **A. Roald Dahl**
☐ **B. Lewis Carroll**
☐ **C. Dr. Seuss**
☐ **D. J.R.R. Tolkien**

2. Which Charles Dickens novel was originally given the "guaranteed instant classic" title *Tom-All-Alone's Factory That Got Into Chancery and Never Got Out*?

☐ **A.** *Bleak House*
☐ **B.** *Great Expectations*
☐ **C.** *A Christmas Carol*
☐ **D.** *The Pickwick Papers*

☐ **A. Merriam-Webster's Dictionary**
☐ **B.** *Joy of Cooking*
☐ **C.** *Guinness Book of World Records*
☐ **D. Roget's Thesaurus**

3. *What book is the volume most commonly stolen from libraries around the world?*

ANSWERS

1. **C.** Prescient as always, Seuss portrayed his nerd with rumpled hair and a black t-shirt in the 1950 book *If I Ran the Zoo.*

2. **A.** With the original title, the book's sales numbers would have been *Bleak* indeed.

3. **C.** *The record holder holds a record—now that's meta!*

QUESTIONS

4. What book does not contain a single letter "e"?

- [ ] A. *Gadsby* by Ernest Wright
- [ ] B. *To Kill a Mockingbird* by Harper Lee
- [ ] C. *Catch-22* by Joseph Heller
- [ ] D. *Lolita* by Vladimir Nabokov

5. *Which is* not *one of the Brontë sisters?*

- [ ] A. Anne
- [ ] B. Charlotte
- [ ] C. Emily
- [ ] D. Elizabeth

6. Which is *not* the first line of a famous novel?

- [ ] A. "Marley was dead, to begin with. There is no doubt whatever about that."
- [ ] B. "Anderson had enjoyed ten years of being totally irresponsible."
- [ ] C. "When he was nearly thirteen, my brother Jem got his arm badly broken at the elbow."
- [ ] D. "It was a pleasure to burn."

ANSWERS

4. **A.** The 1939 book's subtitle offers a helpful hint: *A Story of Over 50,000 Words Without Using the Letter "E."*

5. **D.** *Each sister was a famous novelist in her own right, but they "burst" onto the literary scene together with a book of poetry under the pen names Currier, Ellis, and Acton Bell—and the book sold a whopping two copies.*

6. **B.** The others are from Charles Dickens's *A Christmas Carol*, Harper Lee's *To Kill a Mockingbird*, and Ray Bradbury's *Fahrenheit 451*.

QUESTIONS

7. Which opera tells the story of a nobleman with an eye for the ladies who is ultimately punished by being sent to hell?

☐ **A.** *Tosca*
☐ **B.** *La Traviata*
☐ **C.** *Don Giovanni*
☐ **D.** *La Bohème*

8. If you take a trip to the capital with Effie Trinket, where are you likely to be going?

☐ **A. Panem**
☐ **B. Oz**
☐ **C. Middle-Earth**
☐ **D. Narnia**

☐ **A.** *The Poky Little Puppy*
☐ **B.** *The Little Red Hen*
☐ **C.** *This Little Piggy*
☐ **D.** *Three Little Kittens*

9. *What is the best-selling Little Golden Book of all time?*

ANSWERS

7. **C.** *Mozart's hero is better known by the translation of his name, Don Juan.*

8. **A.** You are likely to be headed into the Arena with the other tributes in Suzanne Collins's best-selling *Hunger Games* trilogy. But be careful: Twenty-four tributes enter, but only one can leave!

A. More than 15 million copies of this classic book have sold since it was first published in September 1942. **9.**

QUESTIONS

10. In the book series *Percy Jackson and the Olympians*, Camp Half-Blood is a place that welcomes what?

- ☐ **A. Mythological monsters**
- ☐ **B. Demigods**
- ☐ **C. Humans**
- ☐ **D. The dead**

11. *The late 1970s TV show* Shields and Yarnell *was a showcase for what performance art?*

- ☐ **A. Break dance**
- ☐ **B. Sculpture**
- ☐ **C. Mime**
- ☐ **D. Yarn bombing**

12. Which writer was commissioned by President Bill Clinton to write a poem for his 1993 inauguration?

- ☐ **A. Maya Angelou**
- ☐ **B. Gwendolyn Brooks**
- ☐ **C. Rita Dove**
- ☐ **D. Louise Gluck**

ANSWERS

B. *Percy Jackson and his fellow campers are all demigods—having one human and one god for parents.*

10.

11. **C.** Mimes Robert Shields and Lorene Yarnell were married in a mime wedding in Union Square and went on to win an Emmy for their television program.

12. **A.** Angelou wrote "On the Pulse of the Morning" for the occasion.

QUESTIONS

13. Which artist painted *The Persistence of Memory*, a surrealist work featuring melting timepieces?

A. Vincent van Gogh
B. Salvador Dalí
C. Frida Kahlo
D. Paul Gauguin

A. Professional wrestlers
B. Ballet dancers
C. Competitive swimmers
D. Kings

14. Early comic book artists took inspiration for superheroes' tights and capes from what profession?

15. Which classic Dutch painter chose himself as one of his favorite subjects?

A. Johannes Vermeer
B. Frans Hals
C. Rembrandt van Rijn
D. Jan de Bray

ANSWERS

13. **B.** *And college dorm room walls all over the world are thankful for it!*

To win over his muse, Dalí smeared himself with goat dung, waxed the hair from his armpits and colored them blue, and wore flowers on his head. Unable to resist his approach, the woman responded by becoming his wife and business manager—a partnership that lasted the rest of his life.

14. **A.** Professional wrestlers and circus strongmen in the early twentieth century needed tight outfits for maximum flexibility and visual appeal. The briefs-over-tights look popularized by superheroes was born from necessity: Since Lycra and elastic weren't yet invented, there was a good chance performers could split their tights. As insurance against exposing their "little performers" to the world, they wore trunks over their tights.

15. **C.** *Rembrandt produced around 70 self-portraits—that's a lot of mirror gazing!*

QUESTIONS

16. Who authored the first novel written on a typewriter?

- ☐ **A. Mark Twain**
- ☐ **B. Harriet Beecher Stowe**
- ☐ **C. Louisa May Alcott**
- ☐ **D. Jack London**

---

17. *On which celestial body can you find the Mona Lisa crater, named for the painting by Leonardo da Vinci?*

- ☐ **A. The moon**
- ☐ **B. Mercury**
- ☐ **C. Venus**
- ☐ **D. Mars**

- ☐ **A. Dorothea Lange**
- ☐ **B. Annie Liebovitz**
- ☐ **C. Henri Cartier-Bresson**
- ☐ **D. Ansel Adams**

18. Which photographer is renowned for black and white portraits of natural settings?

ANSWERS

16. **A.** Although there is some debate over exactly which book it was (*The Adventures of Tom Sawyer,* as Twain recalled, or *Life on the Mississippi,* as most scholars agree), Twain wrote in a 1904 letter, "I will now claim—until dispossessed—that I was the first person in the world to apply the type-machine to literature."

C. *In keeping with the planet's name (Venus was the goddess of love), its craters are all named for women.* **17.**

18. **D.** Adams's photos are particularly important to environmentalists, as they celebrate the beauty of nature and were often featured in Sierra Club publications.

QUESTIONS

19. A cephalophore is an artistic depiction of a saint holding what?

A. Cat
B. Bible
C. Head
D. Cross

20. Vincent van Gogh sold only one painting during his lifetime. What was it?

A. *The Red Vineyard*
B. *Starry Night*
C. *Blossoming Almond Tree*
D. *The Night Café*

A. Stephen King
B. John Grisham
C. Tom Wolfe
D. John Updike

21. *Richard Bachman is the alter ego of which famous author?*

ANSWERS

19. **C.** The saint carries his or her own head as a symbol of having been martyred—which makes halo placement tricky indeed.

A. *The work sold for a mere 400 francs a few months before the painter's death—a far cry from the $82.5 million his* Portrait of Doctor Gachet *sold for in 1990.* **20.**

21. **A.** King chose the name Richard after crime novelist Donald E. Westlake's pseudonym, Richard Stark, and Bachman for the band Bachman-Turner Overdrive. He started writing under the pen name to test whether it was his talent or his name that sold books. He wrote four novels (*Rage, The Long Walk, Roadwork,* and *The Running Man*) before being discovered. King continues to reference his most lifelike creation to this day.

QUESTIONS

22. In Roald Dahl's children's book of the same name, to what does *The BFG* refer?

- [ ] **A. Belly Flop Gang**
- [ ] **B. Best Friends Guild**
- [ ] **C. Brain Freeze Gulp**
- [ ] **D. Big Friendly Giant**

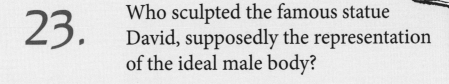

23. Who sculpted the famous statue David, supposedly the representation of the ideal male body?

- [ ] **A. Botticelli**
- [ ] **B. Michelangelo**
- [ ] **C. Francesco da Sangallo**
- [ ] **D. Leonardo da Vinci**

- [ ] **A. Keith Haring**
- [ ] **B. David Hockney**
- [ ] **C. Roy Lichtenstein**
- [ ] **D. Andy Warhol**

24. *Which American pop artist is known for his paintings that resemble large comic strips?*

ANSWERS

22. **D.** Standing 24 feet tall, the BFG's main job was to deliver good dreams to children. He first appeared in Dahl's *Danny, the Champion of the World.* Too bad he didn't show up in Dahl's James Bond script *You Only Live Twice.*

23. **B.** *Take that, Mike "the Situation." You may think you have abs of steel, but David has equally well-sculpted abs of marble—and he's more than 500 years old.*

24. **C.** All four are leaders of the pop art movement, but only Lichtenstein created oversize paintings in the style of bold and bright traditional comic strips.

QUESTIONS

25. How did legendary playwright Tennessee Williams (*A Streetcar Named Desire, Cat on a Hot Tin Roof*) die?

- ☐ A. He choked on a bottle cap.
- ☐ B. He drowned in the Mississippi River.
- ☐ C. He fell from a sixth-story window.
- ☐ D. He was stabbed.

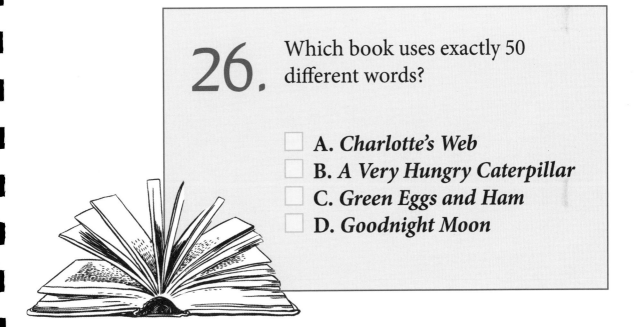

26. Which book uses exactly 50 different words?

- ☐ A. *Charlotte's Web*
- ☐ B. *A Very Hungry Caterpillar*
- ☐ C. *Green Eggs and Ham*
- ☐ D. *Goodnight Moon*

- ☐ A. A canvas
- ☐ B. A piece of pottery
- ☐ C. Skin
- ☐ D. A wall

27. *On which surface would you find a traditional fresco?*

ANSWERS

25. **A.** *Williams, who battled alcoholism and depression for much of his life, died in 1983 at age 71 as a result of choking on the cap from a bottle of eye drops.*

26. **C.** Dr. Seuss's *Green Eggs and Ham*. Seuss's editor bet him he couldn't write a book using 50 words or less. Guess what? The editor lost.

27. **D.** A fresco (which means "fresh" in Italian) is a mural painted on fresh, wet plaster with natural pigments. As the plaster and paint dry, the fresco hardens and becomes permanent. Frescoes are commonly found on church walls.

ANIMALS

1. Which of these dog breeds cannot bark?

- ☐ A. Azawakh
- ☐ B. Basenji
- ☐ C. Catalburun
- ☐ D. Mudi

2. Insect stings kill between 40 and 100 Americans every year. But in other parts of the world, bugs kill many times that number. Which of these critters is responsible for the most human deaths?

- ☐ A. Assassin bug
- ☐ B. Japanese beetle
- ☐ C. Mosquito
- ☐ D. Tsetse fly

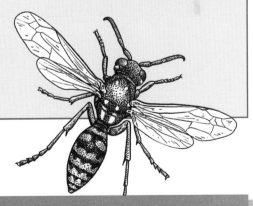

- ☐ A. Elephant
- ☐ B. Howler monkey
- ☐ C. Blue whale
- ☐ D. African lion

3. *Which of these animals has the loudest call?*

ANSWERS

1. **B.** Basenjis, a favorite dog of ancient Egyptians, are incapable of barking. Instead, you'll hear them uttering a sound called a yodel. Azawakhs (African sight hounds), catalburuns (Turkish pointers that are readily identified by their "split-nose"), and mudis (Hungarian herding dogs) all make themselves heard with traditional barks.

2. **C.** *Believe it or not, mosquitoes are responsible for more deaths than any other creature in the world. They spread a wide variety of potentially deadly diseases, including malaria, which kills an estimated two million people a year.*

3. **C.** The call of the blue whale registers an incredible 188 decibels, making it the loudest animal on Earth. Hey, if you had to search the entire ocean for a mate, you'd speak up too!

QUESTIONS

4. How many different dogs played the title role of the television show *Lassie?*

- ☐ **A. 9**
- ☐ **B. 11**
- ☐ **C. 6**
- ☐ **D. 4**

5. *About 20 times a day in the United States, birds and airplanes collide. What's the industry term for the gooey aftermath of such a crash?*

- ☐ **A. Ploogie**
- ☐ **B. Nardle**
- ☐ **C. Malpom**
- ☐ **D. Snarge**

6. Which of the following is *not* a poisonous snake?

- ☐ **A. Viper**
- ☐ **B. Viperine**
- ☐ **C. Eastern Brown Snake**
- ☐ **D. Black Mamba**

ANSWERS

4. **A.** In its 20-year run, 9 different collies helped extricate Timmy and other kids from perilous situations involving bodies of water, cliffs, quicksand, and mine shafts—though never from a well.

5. **D.** *Snarge is no joke! The U.S. Air Force alone spends about $60 million per year repairing damage caused by close encounters of the winged kind.*

B. Viperines aren't poisonous snakes, but they play them on TV . . . or, you know, in the wild. When in danger, these harmless snakes ward off enemies by flattening their heads into a triangle shape that mimics those of their more venomous brethren. **6.**

QUESTIONS

7. Many kinds of caterpillars have evolved to develop a unique camouflage. What material do their bodies emulate?

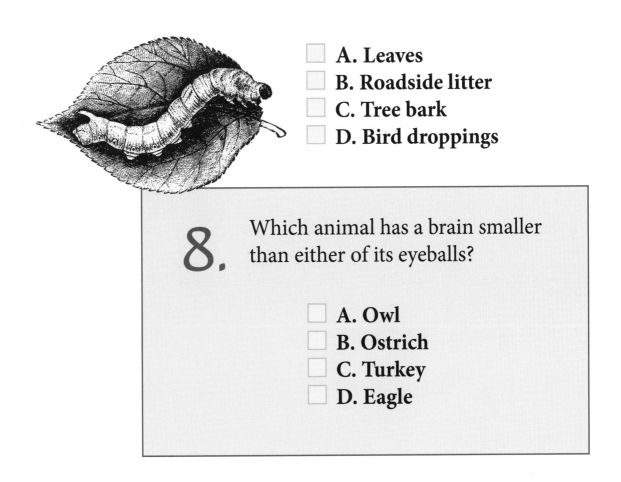

- ☐ **A. Leaves**
- ☐ **B. Roadside litter**
- ☐ **C. Tree bark**
- ☐ **D. Bird droppings**

8. Which animal has a brain smaller than either of its eyeballs?

- ☐ **A. Owl**
- ☐ **B. Ostrich**
- ☐ **C. Turkey**
- ☐ **D. Eagle**

- ☐ **A. Cougars**
- ☐ **B. Bears**
- ☐ **C. Bulldogs**
- ☐ **D. Eagles**

9. *Which animals are most frequently "honored" as mascots at four-year colleges?*

ANSWERS

7. **D.** Sometimes the best defense is a really compelling argument: "Don't eat me, I taste like poo!"

8. **B.** *Ostriches are super-fast (they can run up to 45 miles per hour!) but their small brain size may explain why they are still an easy target for predators: They tend to run in circles.*

D. With 74 teams bearing it as a symbol, the eagle soars to victory. Bulldogs rank third with 39, bears seventh with 30, and cougars ninth with 27. **9.**

QUESTIONS

10. What back-from-the-brink-of-extinction species is nicknamed the "Pig Whistle"?

☐ **A. Javan rhino**
☐ **B. Northern hairy-nosed wombat**
☐ **C. Vancouver Island marmot**
☐ **D. Dwarf blue sheep**

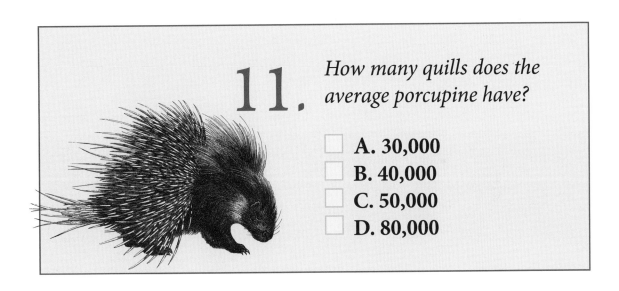

11. How many quills does the average porcupine have?

☐ **A. 30,000**
☐ **B. 40,000**
☐ **C. 50,000**
☐ **D. 80,000**

☐ **A. Butterflies**
☐ **B. Dogs**
☐ **C. Penguins**
☐ **D. Zebras**

12. Macaroni, gentoo, chinstrap, and rock-hopper are types of what?

ANSWERS

10. **C.** Vancouver Island marmots have five distinct whistles, but the one that earned them their nickname is a loud, piercing whistle that sounds the alarm for a nearby predator.

One of the biggest challenges marmots face in keeping their numbers up is that females don't hit puberty until they are 3 or 4. That's a lot of time to spend avoiding predators! The good news is that if they make it to old age (10+), they might have between 12 and 15 pups.

A. And each is a sharp reminder that if you poke at a porcupine, it will poke you back. **11.**

12. **C.** *There are 17 breeds of penguins in the world; these are just four of them.*

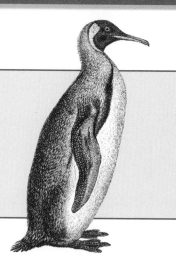

QUESTIONS

13. The pangolin, a toothless mammal found in southern Africa and Asia, is the only mammal to have which of the following reptilian characteristics?

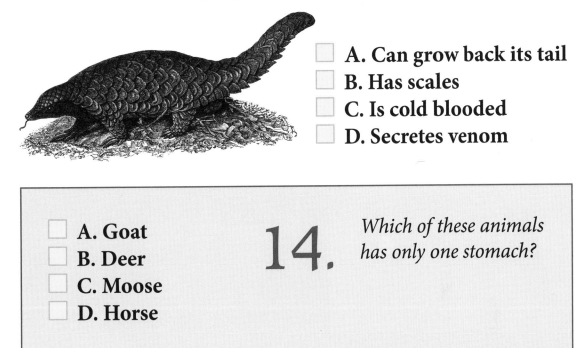

☐ **A. Can grow back its tail**
☐ **B. Has scales**
☐ **C. Is cold blooded**
☐ **D. Secretes venom**

☐ **A. Goat**
☐ **B. Deer**
☐ **C. Moose**
☐ **D. Horse**

14. *Which of these animals has only one stomach?*

15. *A mature ewe yields between 7 and 10 pounds of shorn wool per year. This is, coincidentally, the amount needed to do what?*

☐ **A. Line a pair of Uggs**
☐ **B. Make a man's suit**
☐ **C. Weave an area rug**
☐ **D. Cover the playing surface of a pool table**

ANSWERS

13. **B.** *The pangolin, sometimes referred to as the scaly anteater, is the only mammal with scales. It has no teeth, and uses its powerful claws to tear open termite and ant mounds.*

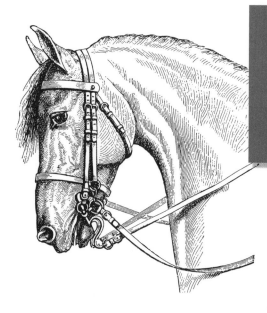

14. **D.** The others are ruminants, animals with four digestive chambers.

When cows and other ruminants eat, the food goes through two digestive chambers, and then travels back up to the mouth, where it is chewed and swallowed again before passing through the last two chambers. The original slow food movement!

15. **B.** But when it comes to the choice of necktie, bowtie, or cravat, you'll have to suit yourself.

QUESTIONS

16. Where did the Manx cat originate?

- ☐ **A. Hawaii**
- ☐ **B. Australia**
- ☐ **C. Isle of Man**
- ☐ **D. Cuba**

17. *Which of these big cats cannot roar?*

- ☐ **A. Lions**
- ☐ **B. Tigers**
- ☐ **C. Leopards**
- ☐ **D. Cheetahs**

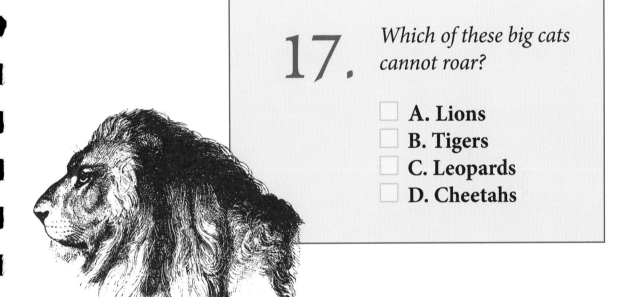

- ☐ **A. Kangaroo**
- ☐ **B. Tasmanian devil**
- ☐ **C. Koala**
- ☐ **D. Possum**

18. Which marsupial can give birth to more live babies than any other species?

ANSWERS

16. **C.** The Manx's lack of tail is caused by a gene mutation—which sure puts those Teenage Mutant Ninja Turtles to shame!

D. *Cheetahs have more in common with their domesticated small cousins— while they can't roar, they can purr while inhaling and exhaling.* **17.**

18. **B.** After a short 21-day gestation cycle, the Tasmanian devil can give birth to as many as 30 live young at one time. But because a mama Tasmanian devil has only four teats, her babies compete fiercely for milk. Eventually, Mom ends up eating many of her kids . . . whole. Aren't you glad you only got sent to your room?

QUESTIONS

19. What type of animal is a Holstein?

- ☐ **A. Cow**
- ☐ **B. Horse**
- ☐ **C. Pig**
- ☐ **D. Sheep**

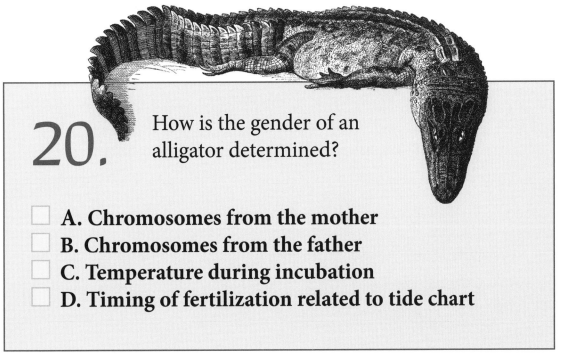

20. How is the gender of an alligator determined?

- ☐ **A. Chromosomes from the mother**
- ☐ **B. Chromosomes from the father**
- ☐ **C. Temperature during incubation**
- ☐ **D. Timing of fertilization related to tide chart**

- ☐ **A. Koala Bear**
- ☐ **B. Kangaroo**
- ☐ **C. Wombat**
- ☐ **D. Possum**
- ☐ **E. Anteater**

21. *Which animal doesn't belong?*

ANSWERS

19. **A.** Got milk? Black-and-white (or sometimes red-and-white) Holsteins are the most popular dairy cows in the United States, making up 90 percent of the total herd.

20. **C.** Alligators lack chromosomes for sex determination. Hot temperatures during incubation produce males, while cooler temperatures produce females.

E. *Anteater. The other four are marsupials, characterized by a pouch in which females carry their young.*

21.

SPORTS

1. Which sport features players using a cesta to throw a pelota at speeds of more than 120 miles per hour?

- ☐ **A. Jai alai**
- ☐ **B. Racquetball**
- ☐ **C. Skeet shooting**
- ☐ **D. Squash**

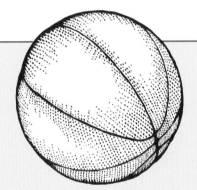

2. What is an NBA player deemed to be if he is awarded the Maurice Podoloff Trophy?

- ☐ **A. Defensive Player of the Year**
- ☐ **B. Most Improved Player**
- ☐ **C. Most Valuable Player**
- ☐ **D. Rookie of the Year**

- ☐ **A. Schwingen**
- ☐ **B. Hornussen**
- ☐ **C. Steinstossen**
- ☐ **D. Waffenlaufen**

3. *Which of these traditional Swiss sports resembles a cross between baseball and golf?*

ANSWERS

1. **A.** Jai alai originated in Spain and is not common in the United States, although it does have a large following in Miami. Because pelotas hit the court walls at such high speeds, each has an average life of only about 20 minutes before its cover splits and it needs to be replaced.

2. **C.** *Podoloff was the first president of the NBA and is the namesake of the league's Most Valuable Player Award.*

3. **B.** Hornussen got its name because of the way the ball buzzes (like a hornet) when it is hit. Schwingen (Alpine wrestling), Steinstossen (stone or boulder throwing), and Waffenlaufen ("weapon running," a sort of armed footrace) are also practiced in Switzerland.

QUESTIONS

4. Which of the following is *not* the name of a baseball pitch?

- [ ] **A. Forkball**
- [ ] **B. Gyroball**
- [ ] **C. Knuckleball**
- [ ] **D. Shovelball**

5. *Who was the first major-league baseball player to have his number retired?*

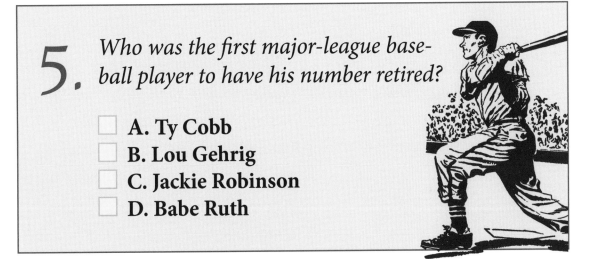

- [ ] **A. Ty Cobb**
- [ ] **B. Lou Gehrig**
- [ ] **C. Jackie Robinson**
- [ ] **D. Babe Ruth**

6. On July 23, 1963, Jimmy Piersall hit his 100th career homer. What did he do on the field to mark this milestone?

- [ ] **A. Ran the bases backward**
- [ ] **B. Turned a cartwheel between second and third base**
- [ ] **C. Skipped from first to second**
- [ ] **D. Ran the diamond with both fists raised in victory**

ANSWERS

4. **D.** A forkball is a type of fastball, and a knuckleball is a unique trick pitch that's more pushed than thrown. A gyroball is a type of pitch in which the ball spins on an axis, much like a spiral pass in football.

5. **B.** *Gehrig wore number 4 for the New York Yankees. The team retired his number on July 4, 1939, after he announced his retirement and diagnosis of amyotrophic lateral sclerosis (ALS).*

6. **A.** When Mets teammate Duke Snyder hit his 400th home run earlier that season, Piersall bet that he could get more publicity for his 100th than Snyder. Guess who collected on that one?

An American baseball uses exactly 108 stitches.

QUESTIONS

7. Which curling term refers to water drops that are sprayed on the ice to make the game more challenging?

- [ ] A. Pebble
- [ ] B. Hack
- [ ] C. Bonspiel
- [ ] D. Hammer

8. Which baseball team was at the center of the scandal in the film *Eight Men Out*?

- [ ] A. Boston Red Sox
- [ ] B. Brooklyn Dodgers
- [ ] C. Chicago Cubs
- [ ] D. Chicago White Sox

9. *Which of these college football bowl games was played more than once?*

- [ ] A. Aluminum Bowl (Little Rock, Arkansas)
- [ ] B. Cement Bowl (Allentown, Pennsylvania)
- [ ] C. Glass Bowl (Toledo, Ohio)
- [ ] D. Salad Bowl (Phoenix, Arizona)

ANSWERS

7. **A.** Hack is a foot brace the curlers push off from; bonspiel refers to a curling tournament; and the hammer is the name for the advantageous last rock of the end.

8. **D.** *The 1919 scandal, known as the Black Sox, occurred when eight members of the White Sox conspired with mobsters to intentionally lose the World Series to the Cincinnati Reds.*

9. **D.** Inexplicably, the Salad Bowl was played in five consecutive seasons (1948–1952); the others were one-hit wonders.

QUESTIONS

10. Which sewing term is *not* common on the football field?

- ☐ **A. Patterns**
- ☐ **B. Buttonhooks**
- ☐ **C. Stitches**
- ☐ **D. Seams**

11. *Which tennis player defeated Bobby Riggs in the 1973 "Battle of the Sexes"?*

- ☐ **A. Martina Navratilova**
- ☐ **B. Billie Jean King**
- ☐ **C. Chris Evert**
- ☐ **D. Margaret Court**

- ☐ **A. Steffi Graff**
- ☐ **B. Magdalena Maleeva**
- ☐ **C. Gabriela Sabatini**
- ☐ **D. Monica Seles**

12. Which tennis player was viciously stabbed while playing a match in Hamburg, Germany, in 1993?

ANSWERS

10. **C.** Though *we're* in stitches thinking about burly football players sitting in a sewing circle!

11. **B.** *Four muscular men costumed as Cleopatra's slaves carried out King on a litter; Riggs came in on a rickshaw pulled by female models wearing suggestive outfits. In the end, this was a good thing, since Riggs could be picked up from the floor (after King wiped it with him) and hauled out on the rickshaw he came in on.*

12. **D.** An obsessed fan of Steffi Graf stabbed Seles in the back with a 9-inch boning knife during a quarterfinals match against Maleeva. Seles recovered from her wounds after a few weeks, but she didn't return to competitive tennis for two years.

QUESTIONS

13. Who was the first hockey player to be honored by *Sports Illustrated* as "Sportsman of the Year"?

- A. Bobby Orr
- B. Wayne Gretzky
- C. Mike Bossy
- D. Guy Lafleur

- A. Mike Eruzione
- B. Mark Johnson
- C. Rob McClanahan
- D. Dave Silk

14. *Who scored the winning goal for the U.S. men's hockey team in the "Miracle on Ice" game against the Soviet Union in the 1980 Olympics?*

15. *Which sports announcer trademarked the catchphrase "Let's get ready to rumble!"?*

- A. Harry Caray
- B. Al Michaels
- C. Michael Buffer
- D. Howard Cosell

ANSWERS

13. **A.** *Orr, who was only 22 at the time, had already had his nose broken three or four times and had injuries requiring 50 or so stitches—Frankenstein in the making!*

14. **A.** Eruzione was the team captain. His winning goal—one of the most played highlights in American sports—was voted the greatest highlight of all time by ESPN viewers in 2008.

15. **C.** Buffer got sports fans rumble-ready for boxing and other matches and has made guest appearances on *The Simpsons* and *South Park* promoting the phrase.

QUESTIONS

16. Which professional wrestler had a costarring role in the film *The Princess Bride?*

☐ **A. Andre the Giant**
☐ **B. Hulk Hogan**
☐ **C. Randy "Macho Man" Savage**
☐ **D. Jesse "The Body" Ventura**

17. *What was the original name of the Nike corporation?*

☐ **A. Apollo Sports**
☐ **B. Blue Ribbon Sports**
☐ **C. Gold Medal Sports**
☐ **D. Olympia Sports**

☐ **A. Going to Disneyland**
☐ **B. Buying a round of drinks for the other 45,000 runners**
☐ **C. Getting married at the finish line**
☐ **D. Giving birth**

18. After finishing the 2011 Chicago Marathon, Amber Miller famously celebrated by doing what?

ANSWERS

16. **A.** Though Ventura went on to become governor of Minnesota, the 7 foot 4, 500-pound Andre the Giant stole the show as Fezzik in the classic movie.

B. *In 1971 the founders of the small sports-shoe business Blue Ribbon Sports in Beaverton, Oregon, were searching for a catchy, energetic company name. They settled on Nike, the name of the Greek goddess of victory. And victorious they were: Nike is now the largest sportswear manufacturer in the world.* **17.**

18. **D.** Talk about an endurance event! Miller and her husband finished the race in 6.5 hours (her contractions started halfway through), had a meal, then went to the hospital, where baby June was born just hours later.

QUESTIONS

19. What decade saw the most Triple Crown winners in horse racing?

- [ ] **A. 1910s**
- [ ] **B. 1930s**
- [ ] **C. 1940s**
- [ ] **D. 1970s**

20. What is known as a "double-double" in Olympic diving?

- [ ] **A. Four dives with perfect scores**
- [ ] **B. Consecutive gold medals in four Olympic Games**
- [ ] **C. Back-to-back gold in springboard and platform**
- [ ] **D. Four gold medals in a single Olympic Games**

- [ ] **A. Rick Barry**
- [ ] **B. Julius Erving**
- [ ] **C. Michael Jordan**
- [ ] **D. Jerry West**

21. *The NBA's logo features a silhouette of a player dribbling a basketball. Which basketball legend is the image modeled on?*

ANSWERS

19. **C.** Whirlaway (1941), Count Fleet (1943), Assault (1946), and Citation (1948).

The last horse to bring home the elusive Triple Crown was American Pharoah (2015), the first since Affirmed (1978).

20. **C.** A "double-double" is back-to-back gold in springboard and platform.

21. **D.** *Although the NBA declines to comment on the identity of the player, the logo's designer is not so reserved. He says he originally designed 40 or 50 options, every one of which featured "Mr. Clutch" (West).*

QUESTIONS

22. What football team made *Billboard's* Top 100 with "The Super Bowl Shuffle" in 1986?

- ☐ **A. Chicago Bears**
- ☐ **B. Denver Broncos**
- ☐ **C. New England Patriots**
- ☐ **D. Pittsburgh Steelers**

- ☐ **A. Muhammad Ali**
- ☐ **B. Charles Barkley**
- ☐ **C. Reggie Jackson**
- ☐ **D. Babe Ruth**

23. *Which famous athlete not-so-humbly claimed, "When you are as great as I am, it's hard to be humble"?*

24. *What do sumo wrestlers throw into the ring prior to a match?*

- ☐ **A. Powder**
- ☐ **B. Rice**
- ☐ **C. Salt**
- ☐ **D. Nothing**

ANSWERS

22. **A.** "Punky QB" Jim McMahon, Walter Payton, and William "Refrigerator" Perry were among those in the Super Bowl-winning "Shufflin' Crew" who rapped and danced their way onto the charts. Proceeds from the song were donated to charity.

A. *Not only could the champion boxer float like a butterfly and sting like a bee, but he was also a champion boaster.* **23.**

"At home I am a nice guy, but I don't want the world to know. Humble people, I've found, don't get very far."
—Muhammad Ali

24. **C.** Sumo wrestlers throw several handfuls of salt into the ring as a purifying ritual. Some will also sprinkle salt around their bodies, as a way of protecting themselves from injury.

Sumo wrestling is Japan's national sport.

QUESTIONS

25. Which athlete has *not* been featured on a Wheaties cereal box?

A. "Stone Cold" Steve Austin (professional wrestler)
B. Rulon Gardner (Olympic Greco-Roman wrestler)
C. Joe Paterno (college football coach)
D. Esther Williams (swimmer; actress)

26. *Which of the following pro football-playing brothers are twins?*

A. Ronde and Tiki Barber
B. Eli and Peyton Manning
C. Adrian and Mike Peterson
D. Byron and Brian Westbrook

A. The Golden Bear
B. The Great White Shark
C. The Hawk
D. The King

27. What is golfer Arnold Palmer's nickname?

ANSWERS

25. **B.** Gardner never muscled his way onto the box, but Austin, Paterno, and Williams graced breakfast tables across America in 1999, 2003, and 1959, respectively.

26. **A.** The Barber boys are identical twins—and they're not related to the NFL's other Barber brothers, Marion and Dominique.

27. **D.** *The most popular golfer of all time, Arnie is known by millions of fans (dubbed "Arnie's Army") simply as "The King." If you've heard the other monikers but can't tie them to their owners, here you go: Jack Nicklaus is the Golden Bear, Greg Norman is the Great White Shark, and Ben Hogan was the Hawk.*

QUESTIONS

28. Which of the following drivers did *not* win the Indianapolis 500 four times?

☐ **A. Mario Andretti**
☐ **B. A.J. Foyt**
☐ **C. Rick Mears**
☐ **D. Al Unser**

☐ **A. Champagne**
☐ **B. Apple cider**
☐ **C. Milk**
☐ **D. Bourbon**

29. *What beverage does the winner of the Indy 500 traditionally drink in victory lane?*

30. *Throwing one no-hitter is tough enough, but which major-league pitcher tossed back-to-back no-hitters in 1938?*

☐ **A. Carl Hubbell**
☐ **B. Hoyt Wilhelm**
☐ **C. Johnny Vander Meer**
☐ **D. Lefty Gomez**

ANSWERS

28. **A.** For all his many other accomplishments, Andretti won the Indy 500 just once. The others listed share the record with four Indy 500 victories.

C. *After three-time winner Louis Meyer drank buttermilk in victory lane in 1936, a dairy-industry executive made a pitch to keep the tradition going and it caught on.* **29.**

30. **C.** Vander Meer, a Cincinnati Reds left-hander, no-hit the Boston Braves and Brooklyn Dodgers in consecutive games. His unprecedented second straight "no-no," on June 15 at Ebbets Field, was also the first night baseball game in New York City.

QUESTIONS

31. Who is the only player ever named NCAA Final Four MVP three times?

☐ **A. Bill Walton**
☐ **B. Elvin Hayes**
☐ **C. Lewis Alcindor**
☐ **D. Michael Jordan**

---

32. *Who made the winning shot in North Carolina's 1982 NCAA title game victory over Georgetown?*

☐ **A. Michael Jordan**
☐ **B. James Worthy**
☐ **C. Jimmy Black**
☐ **D. Phil Ford**

☐ **A. Bill Walton**
☐ **B. Jerry West**
☐ **C. Bob Cousy**
☐ **D. Kevin McHale**

33. Which of these greats is not in the Basketball Hall of Fame for his role with the Boston Celtics?

ANSWERS

31. **C.** Lewis Alcindor, before he became known as Kareem Abdul-Jabbar, was honored as MVP in 1967, '68, and '69.

A. *Jordan, just a freshman at the time, launched a long career of clutch shooting and winning championships when his 17-footer led the Tar Heels to victory.* **32.**

33. **B.** While the others are Boston Celtics Hall of Famers, West starred for the rival Los Angeles Lakers.

HISTORY

1. What was the end result of the Manhattan Project?

- ☐ A. An atomic bomb
- ☐ B. The Brooklyn Bridge
- ☐ C. A hovercraft
- ☐ D. The Flux Capacitor

2. What did Al Capone go to jail for?

- ☐ A. Extortion
- ☐ B. Mail fraud
- ☐ C. Tax evasion
- ☐ D. Murder

- ☐ A. Cimarron, New Mexico
- ☐ B. Cripple Creek, Colorado
- ☐ C. Dodge City, Kansas
- ☐ D. Tombstone, Arizona

3. *Which town was the scene of the Gunfight at the O.K. Corral?*

ANSWERS

1. **A.** The project lasted from 1942 to early 1947 and took place simultaneously in more than 30 cities in the United States, Canada, and the United Kingdom. Manhattan was the first headquarters of the top-secret project—right across from city hall.

2. **C.** *Despite all his alleged wrongdoings, he was only ever convicted of income tax evasion in 1931 and sentenced to 11 years in prison. Capone was paroled in 1939 and succumbed to a heart attack in 1947. Death and taxes.*

3. **D.** Actually, the famous gunfight between Wyatt Earp's crew and a group of outlaw brothers took place *near* the O.K. Corral, in an empty lot next to Camillus Fly's photography studio. Perhaps "Gunfight at the C.F. Studio" wasn't catchy enough.

QUESTIONS

4. What age followed the Bronze Age?

- ☐ **A. Ice Age**
- ☐ **B. Iron Age**
- ☐ **C. Stone Age**
- ☐ **D. Age of Innocence**

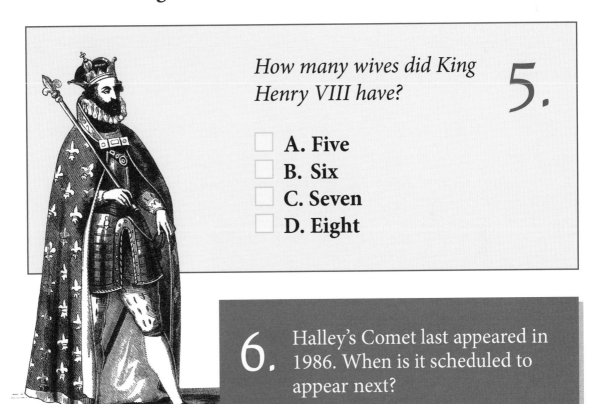

How many wives did King Henry VIII have?

5.

- ☐ **A. Five**
- ☐ **B. Six**
- ☐ **C. Seven**
- ☐ **D. Eight**

6. Halley's Comet last appeared in 1986. When is it scheduled to appear next?

- ☐ **A. 2041**
- ☐ **B. 2048**
- ☐ **C. 2061**
- ☐ **D. 2087**

ANSWERS

4. **B.** Characterized by the types of material being used to make tools at the time, the Stone Age is first in the Three-Age System of archaeology, followed by the Bronze Age, and then the Iron Age. In Hollywood, though, *Ice Age* was followed by *Ice Age: The Meltdown, Ice Age: Dawn of the Dinosaurs,* and *Ice Age: Continental Drift.*

5. **B.** *Henry was married six times. Probably the most famous of his wives was the ill-fated Anne Boleyn, executed in 1536. If you have trouble keeping track of all of Henry's wives, try to remember this little mnemonic device: "Annulled, beheaded, died; annulled, beheaded, survived."*

6. **C.** The comet is visible from Earth every 75 to 76 years as it orbits the sun. American author Mark Twain was born two weeks after the comet's *perihelion* (when it's closest to the sun) in 1835, and he predicted he would live until the comet's return. He died April 21, 1910—the day after the comet's next perihelion.

QUESTIONS

7. What was the name of the theater where President Lincoln was assassinated?

- ☐ **A. Booth Theater**
- ☐ **B. Ford's Theater**
- ☐ **C. Lions Theater**
- ☐ **D. Marquee Theater**

8. *Investment manager Bernie Madoff shocked Wall Street and the world when he was arrested for stealing billions of dollars from investors in a massive financial fraud. What kind of scam was this?*

- ☐ **A. Pyramid scheme**
- ☐ **B. Affinity fraud**
- ☐ **C. Ponzi scheme**
- ☐ **D. Promissory notes**

9. Who famously said, "That's one small step for a man, one giant leap for mankind"?

- ☐ **A. Buzz Aldrin**
- ☐ **B. Neil Armstrong**
- ☐ **C. John Glenn**
- ☐ **D. Buzz Lightyear**

ANSWERS

7. **B.** On the night of April 14, 1865, John Wilkes Booth waited for the main character's big laugh line in Tom Taylor's play *Our American Cousin:* "Don't know the manners of good society, eh? Well, I guess I know enough to turn you inside out, old gal—you sockdologizing old man-trap." The audience's laughter concealed the gunshot. It's probably inappropriate to say you had to be there.

8. *C. Ponzi scheme. U.S. prosecutors estimated that the worldwide scheme eventually totaled $64.8 billion. Madoff pled guilty to 11 criminal charges, including wire fraud, mail fraud, and money laundering. In 2009, he was sentenced to 150 years in prison. Using that length of sentence, he'll repay his duped investors at a rate of $14 per second . . . if he somehow manages to live until 2159.*

9. **B.** Armstrong was the first man to walk on the moon. Later that year, *Apollo 12* astronaut Pete Conrad, shortest member of his astronaut corps, landed on the moon, jumped down from his lunar module, and said, "Whoopie! That may have been a small one for Neil, but it's a long one for me."

QUESTIONS

10. During their expedition across the American West from 1804 to 1806, explorers Meriwether Lewis and William Clark traveled with a French fur trader and his young Shoshone wife. What was her name?

☐ **A. Kateri Tekakwitha**
☐ **B. Pocahontas**
☐ **C. Sacagawea**
☐ **D. Weetamoo**

☐ **A. Prison**
☐ **B. Pelican**
☐ **C. Paradise**
☐ **D. Poet**

11. *Alcatraz Island has a rich history, beginning with its name. Alcatraz is a Spanish word that translates into what?*

12. When Allied troops invaded the beaches of Normandy, France, on June 6, 1944, it went by what code name?

☐ **A. Operation Neptune**
☐ **B. Operation Luna**
☐ **C. Operation Phalanx**
☐ **D. Operation Eclipse**

ANSWERS

10. **C.** Although she did not serve as a guide for the expedition, as is often reported, Sacagawea helped foster diplomacy with Native Americans, provided input on the best routes to take, and served as an interpreter. She was the human version of a modern smartphone.

11. **B.** *Originally considered the "Evil Island" by Native Americans, the "Island of the Pelicans" has been a military garrison, a military prison, the site of a Native American civil rights occupation, and a tourist trap. Operating as a federal prison from 1934 to 1963, Alcatraz housed such notorious figures as Al Capone, Mickey Cohen, and George "Machine Gun" Kelly. Now it's home to the California slender salamander. At least those don't try to escape.*

A. Likely named for the Roman god of the sea, Operation Neptune succeeded after elaborate deceptions led Adolf Hitler to believe that Allied forces planned to attack from the Straits of Dover. That operation was called Operation Bodyguard. No guessing where that name came from! **12.**

QUESTIONS

13. The War of 1812 occurred between which two nations?

- ☐ **A. France and Spain**
- ☐ **B. Russia and the British Empire**
- ☐ **C. The British Empire and the United States**
- ☐ **D. France and Russia**

14. *According to the Supreme Court decision in the case of* Brown v. Board of Education, *the* Plessy v. Ferguson *decision violated which amendment by upholding racial segregation in public schools?*

- ☐ **A. First Amendment**
- ☐ **B. Eleventh Amendment**
- ☐ **C. Twelfth Amendment**
- ☐ **D. Fourteenth Amendment**

- ☐ **A. 16 months**
- ☐ **B. 24 weeks**
- ☐ **C. 32 days**
- ☐ **D. 40 minutes**

15. *How long was the shortest war in history?*

ANSWERS

13. **C.** *All these pairings were at war with each other in 1812, due to a little emperor named Napoleon. Ultimately, the 32-month Revolutionary War rematch resolved the remaining concerns over the United States' declaration of independence, and the U.S. and the U.K. have been close allies ever since.*

14. **D.** The Equal Protection Clause of the Fourteenth Amendment states, "No state shall . . . deny to any person within its jurisdiction the equal protection of the laws." The Fifteenth Amendment ultimately allowed everyone to vote. (Except women—that happened 50 years later.)

15. **D.** After the pro-British sultan of Zanzibar died in 1896, a not-so-pro-British sultan took his place. The United Kingdom issued an ultimatum that resulted in a 40-minute war. Zanzibar took 500 casualties while Britain took just one. Another pro-British sultan assumed leadership of the puppet government, and Britain controlled Zanzibar for the next 67 years.

QUESTIONS

16. Which war do the movies *Apocalypse Now, Full Metal Jacket, Hamburger Hill,* and *Platoon* depict?

- ☐ **A. Vietnam War**
- ☐ **B. Korean War**
- ☐ **C. Peloponnesian War**
- ☐ **D. Crimean War**

17. *What famous world event happened on November 9, 1989?*

- ☐ **A. The TV show *Seinfeld* premiered**
- ☐ **B. The Berlin Wall fell**
- ☐ **C. Ayatollah Khomeini died**
- ☐ **D. Tiananmen Square massacre occurred**

- ☐ **A. Map out pyramid interiors**
- ☐ **B. Flatten wet papyrus**
- ☐ **C. Translate ancient text**
- ☐ **D. Find Mt. Olympus**

18. The Rosetta Stone is an important artifact because it allowed historians to do what?

ANSWERS

16. **A.** Including *Good Morning, Vietnam* would have made it too easy.

B. *What a big year in history 1989 happened to be. All of these events occurred in 1989, but the toppling of the Berlin Wall and reunification of Germany began on November 9. British Prime Minister Margaret Thatcher begged Soviet President Mikhail Gorbachev not to let it happen because she feared the worst for Europe.*

17.

18. **C.** The carved stone contained text written in three different ancient languages. Using their knowledge of the Greek text, linguists were able to translate the stone's older Egyptian writings and hieroglyphs. Think of it as a 1,700-pound decoder ring. The original translator app.

QUESTIONS

19. Who was the only president to get married in the White House?

- A. Martin Van Buren
- B. Grover Cleveland
- C. James A. Garfield
- D. Warren G. Harding

20. Under presidential succession law, who is next in line for the presidency after the vice president and the Speaker of the House?

- A. President pro tempore of the Senate
- B. Secretary of state
- C. Secretary of defense
- D. Secretary of the Treasury

- A. Andrew Johnson
- B. James K. Polk
- C. Richard Nixon
- D. Bill Clinton

21. *Who was the first U.S. president to be impeached?*

ANSWERS

19. **B.** Another noteworthy "one and only" fact about the man on the $1,000 bill: He's the only president to serve two non-consecutive terms. Cleveland was the 22nd and 24th president of the United States of America.

20. **A.** When President Andrew Johnson was impeached in 1868, he had no vice president—Senate president pro tempore Benjamin Franklin Wade was next in line. Wade was a radical, and historians believe that Johnson was tried and acquitted mostly to keep Wade out of the White House. Shortly afterward, the Speaker and president pro tempore were removed from the line of succession. When they were ultimately restored in 1947, the Speaker and president pro tempore were placed third and fourth, respectively.

21. **A.** *Johnson was Abraham Lincoln's vice president and succeeded Lincoln following his assassination. Johnson was impeached by the House of Representatives, though the act failed in the U.S. Senate. (Remember question #20?) Johnson was impeached for violating the Tenure of Office Act that had been enacted the year before, which he vetoed and Congress passed anyway.*

MUSIC

1. Which fairy tale inspired Duran Duran's hit song "Hungry Like the Wolf"?

- A. *The Wolf and the Seven Little Kids*
- B. *The Three Little Pigs*
- C. *The Wolf and the Man*
- D. *Little Red Riding Hood*

2. Metallica's 1990s smash hit "Enter Sandman" features the repeating lyric "We're off to never-never land." What lyric did singer James Hetfield originally write instead of this catchphrase?

- A. "Maybe it's not meant to be"
- B. "Disrupt the perfect family"
- C. "Dream in perfect ecstasy"
- D. "Nightmares help you really see"

3. *In the Simon and Garfunkel song of the same name, why does the narrator need to go "Somewhere They Can't Find Me"?*

- A. He had a fight with his brother.
- B. He robbed a liquor store.
- C. He escaped from prison.
- D. His lover broke his heart.

ANSWERS

1. **D.** "Hungry Like the Wolf" was the second single from the 1982 album *Rio*.

2. **B.** *The band decided the lyric was too dark for the song to succeed and convinced Hetfield to change it—and the rest, as they say, is RIAA Certified Platinum single history.*

B. The narrator leaves his lover in the middle of the night to avoid being arrested. **3.**

QUESTIONS

4. What patriotically titled album was the first compact disc ever made in the United States?

- [ ] A. *Breakfast in America,* Supertramp
- [ ] B. *America (The Way I See It),* Hank Williams, Jr.
- [ ] C. *Born in the U.S.A.,* Bruce Springsteen
- [ ] D. *Back in the USA,* MC5

Who was the inspiration for the dude in Aerosmith's "Dude (Looks Like a Lady)"?

5.

- [ ] A. Vince Neil (Mötley Crüe)
- [ ] B. Jon Bon Jovi (Bon Jovi)
- [ ] C. Dee Snider (Twisted Sister)
- [ ] D. Sebastian Bach (Skid Row)

---

6. *Which holiday is described in Chicago's 1972 hit "Saturday in the Park"?*

- [ ] A. Easter
- [ ] B. Christmas
- [ ] C. Memorial Day
- [ ] D. Fourth of July

ANSWERS

4. **C.** The Boss's 1984 release shares the record for most top ten hits (seven) from a single album with *Thriller* (Michael Jackson, 1982) and *Rhythm Nation 1814* (Janet Jackson, 1989).

5. **A.** *The song was released in 1987 at the height of the "hair bands." Go ahead, Google it. We'll wait.*

D. Can you dig it? Yes, we can. **6.**

QUESTIONS

7. Who is the only male country music star to have exceeded 10 million sales for four different albums?

- ☐ **A. Johnny Cash**
- ☐ **B. Garth Brooks**
- ☐ **C. Willie Nelson**
- ☐ **D. Kenny Chesney**

8. *Which of these musical acts turned down the chance to perform at the 1969 Woodstock Music and Art Festival?*

- ☐ **A. The Grateful Dead**
- ☐ **B. Sly & the Family Stone**
- ☐ **C. Jethro Tull**
- ☐ **D. Jefferson Airplane**

9. Which band did *not* feature legendary guitarist Eric Clapton?

- ☐ **A. The Yardbirds**
- ☐ **B. Traffic**
- ☐ **C. Cream**
- ☐ **D. Derek and the Dominos**

ANSWERS

7. **B.** Perhaps his "Friends in Low Places" were hanging out at the record shop.

8. **C.** *In an interview, front man Ian Anderson cited his aversion to hippies and spontaneous outdoor nudity as reasons for turning down the gig.*

B. Steve Winwood, who formed Traffic with three friends, later went on to form the band Blind Faith with Clapton. **9.**

QUESTIONS

10. Ozzy Osbourne was famously banned from the city of San Antonio for a decade. What did he do to earn his banishment?

- ☐ **A. Bit the head off a live bat in a concert there**
- ☐ **B. Gave a lewd, nude public performance**
- ☐ **C. Urinated on the Alamo**
- ☐ **D. Started a riot**

11. *Which of these musicians is not a native Canadian?*

- ☐ **A. Alanis Morissette**
- ☐ **B. Neil Young**
- ☐ **C. Celine Dion**
- ☐ **D. Van Morrison**

12. What American city is most associated with grunge music?

- ☐ **A. New York City**
- ☐ **B. Memphis**
- ☐ **C. Seattle**
- ☐ **D. Minneapolis**

ANSWERS

10. **C.** Osbourne acted in a drunken stupor, but later made up with the city by donating $20,000 to the Daughters of the Republic of Texas to help restore the national landmark. We bet Ozzy doesn't have any trouble remembering the Alamo these days!

11. **D.** *The "Brown-Eyed Girl" singer was born in Belfast, Ireland.*

C. Seattle produced grunge rockers Pearl Jam, Alice in Chains, Soundgarden, and of course, Nirvana. **12.**

QUESTIONS

13. Which piano-playing entertainer earned the nicknames "Mr. Showmanship" and "The Glitter Man"?

- ☐ **A. Stevie Wonder**
- ☐ **B. Liberace**
- ☐ **C. Elton John**
- ☐ **D. Billy Joel**

14. *Which musical genre has the most radio stations in the United States?*

- ☐ **A. Rock**
- ☐ **B. Top 40**
- ☐ **C. Country**
- ☐ **D. Oldies**

- ☐ **A. Vocal cords**
- ☐ **B. Throat**
- ☐ **C. Hands**
- ☐ **D. Fingers**

15. *Music legend Bob Dylan had what body part insured by Lloyd's of London?*

ANSWERS

13. **B.** *Liberace's legendary bedazzled pianos were no match for his wardrobe, which included such gems as a blue fox cape that trailed 16 feet behind him and a King Neptune costume that weighed 200 pounds.*

14. **C.** There are nearly 2,000 country stations around the country. That's a lot of twang!

15. **A.** Dylan was apparently worried that the day would come when he would stop blowin' in the wind.

QUESTIONS

16. Which classic novel was the inspiration for the 1980 Police hit "Don't Stand So Close to Me"?

☐ **A.** *Crime and Punishment*
☐ **B.** *Lolita*
☐ **C.** *Anna Karenina*
☐ **D.** *Doctor Zhivago*

---

17. *Which height-challenged singer was parodied in an infamous basketball skit on* Chappelle's Show?

☐ **A. David Bowie**
☐ **B. Cee Lo Green**
☐ **C. Lil Wayne**
☐ **D. Prince**

☐ **A. George Harrison**
☐ **B. Paul McCartney**
☐ **C. John Lennon**
☐ **D. Ringo Starr**

18. Which former Beatle was the first person to be featured on the cover of *Rolling Stone?*

ANSWERS

16. **B.** The author of *Lolita* is name-checked in the song when Sting sings, "Just like the old man in that book by Nabokov."

17. **D.** *In the skit, Charlie Murphy tells a story about being beaten in basketball by Prince and his crew, who were still wearing their stage costumes (picture a purple velvet suit and heeled boots). After the skit aired, Prince said in interviews that while he wasn't really wearing a costume, he really did school Murphy on the court.*

18. **C.** No, it wasn't the naked picture with Yoko Ono. In 1967, Lennon was featured in a still from the film *How I Won the War*.

TELEVISION

1. In which PBS children's show did a trolley transport viewers to the Neighborhood of Make Believe?

- A. *Sesame Street*
- B. *The Electric Company*
- C. *Mister Rogers' Neighborhood*
- D. *Reading Rainbow*

2. *Which* Girls *cast member does* not *have a famous parent?*

- A. Zosia Mamet
- B. Jemima Kirke
- C. Allison Williams
- D. Lena Dunham

3. He's not a doctor, but he plays them (or tries to) on TV. Which role did Patrick Dempsey audition for before landing the role of McDreamy himself, Dr. Derek Shepherd, on *Grey's Anatomy*?

- A. Dr. Jack Hodgins, *Bones*
- B. Dr. Mark Greene, *ER*
- C. Dr. Robert Chase, *House*
- D. Dr. Sean McNamara, *Nip/Tuck*

ANSWERS

1. **C.** The puppets in the Neighborhood of Make Believe were named for important people in Rogers's life, including Queen Sara Saturday (his wife), Harriet Elizabeth Cow (his aunt), and Lady Elaine Fairchilde (his sister).

Mister Rogers's ubiquitous cardigans were all hand-knit by his mother, Nancy McFeely Rogers. Now that's a special way of saying "I love you."

2. **D.** *Mamet's father is playwright David Mamet; Kirke's father is drummer Simon Kirke; and Williams's father is news anchor Brian Williams.*

3. **C.** Hmm, we're not feeling it. We could see him rocking the role of Dr. Wilson, though.

QUESTIONS

4. Which *Doctor Who* also had a role in *Harry Potter and the Goblet of Fire?*

- ☐ **A. Paul McGann**
- ☐ **B. Christopher Eccleston**
- ☐ **C. David Tennant**
- ☐ **D. Matt Smith**

What was the name of the in-house band on The Muppet Show?

5.

- ☐ **A. Extraordinary Chaos**
- ☐ **B. Electric Mayhem**
- ☐ **C. Eclectic Bedlam**
- ☐ **D. Endearing Pandemonium**

---

6. *Which of these classics is generally considered to be the first reality TV show?*

- ☐ **A.** *Truth or Consequences*
- ☐ **B.** *Candid Camera*
- ☐ **C.** *I've Got a Secret*
- ☐ **D.** *To Tell the Truth*

ANSWERS

4. **C.** Tennant played Barty Crouch, Jr., a wizard who left Hogwarts to join the evil forces of Lord Voldemort.

5. **B.** *Led by Dr. Teeth, the band included Sgt. Floyd Pepper on the bass, Janice on lead guitar and vocals, and, of course, Animal on the drums.*

B. The *Punked* of its day, Allen Funt's hidden camera/practical joke series premiered in 1948. **6.**

QUESTIONS

7. Which game on the long-running show *The Price Is Right* requires contestants to earn chips, then slide them down a pegboard in attempt to land on a big cash prize?

- **A. Showcase Showdown**
- **B. Plinko**
- **C. Pass the Buck**
- **D. Hi Lo**

8. *Which couple were the first to be shown in bed together on primetime American television?*

- **A. Fred and Wilma Flintstone (*The Flintstones*)**
- **B. Mike and Carol Brady (*The Brady Bunch*)**
- **C. Lucy and Ricky Ricardo (*I Love Lucy*)**
- **D. Samantha and Darren Stevens (*Bewitched*)**

9. What are the names of Marge's older sisters on *The Simpsons?*

- **A. Lori and Bertha**
- **B. Annie and Melba**
- **C. Patty and Selma**
- **D. Jackie and Diana**

ANSWERS

7. **B.** The top prize for Plinko is $2,500—unless you are a lucky contestant who "comes on down" during Big Money Week, when the top prize is doubled to $5,000.

The Price Is Right, *which first aired in 1972, is television's longest-running game show.*

8. **A.** *Amazingly enough, the town of Bedrock (and the rest of America) didn't take to the fainting couches in shock at the sight.*

9. **C.** Marge's chain-smoking, Homer-hating twin sisters live together at the Spinster Arms apartment complex and work at the DMV.

QUESTIONS

10. After 15 seasons of sassy TV courtroom drama, CBS canceled which judge's show in 2013 over a salary dispute?

- ☐ **A. Judith Sheindlin** *(Judge Judy)*
- ☐ **B. Greg Mathis** *(Judge Mathis)*
- ☐ **C. Jeanine Pirro** *(Judge Pirro)*
- ☐ **D. Joseph Brown** *(Judge Joe Brown)*

11. *Which British TV series has been nominated for the most Emmy Awards?*

- ☐ **A. *Sherlock***
- ☐ **B. *Doctor Who***
- ☐ **C. *Monty Python's Flying Circus***
- ☐ **D. *Downton Abbey***

12. If you hired the firm Sterling Cooper Draper Pryce, what services would you get?

- ☐ **A. Legal counsel**
- ☐ **B. Crisis management**
- ☐ **C. Advertising**
- ☐ **D. Architecture and design**

ANSWERS

10. **D.** Judge Brown claimed he was promised a salary of $20 million per year but the network didn't pay up. Perhaps he should take them to court . . . *The People's Court.*

11. **D.** *In its first two seasons alone, the period drama was nominated for a whopping 27 Emmys.*

12. **C.** The men and women of *Mad Men* know how to sell a product—especially a cable TV show!

QUESTIONS

13. On which short-lived cartoon did disgraced 1980s pop duo Milli Vanilli make a guest appearance?

☐ **A.** *The Adventures of Super Mario Bros. 3*
☐ **B.** *Bill & Ted's Excellent Adventures*
☐ **C.** *Pole Position*
☐ **D.** *Alf's Animated Adventures*

14. *What fictional company counts Wile E. Coyote among its best customers?*

☐ **A.** Amway
☐ **B.** Acme
☐ **C.** Arrow
☐ **D.** Atlantis

☐ **A.** Ricki Lake
☐ **B.** Maury Povich
☐ **C.** Jerry Springer
☐ **D.** Montel Williams

15. *Which talk show host has cornered the market on public paternity tests, proclaiming dramatically, "You are/are not the father" as the results are revealed?*

ANSWERS

13. **A.** *Rob and Fab were kidnapped by Bowser's minions and brought back to the castle for a command live performance. You can guess how that turned out.*

14. **B.** The shady Acme company specialized in inventions designed to help capture Road Runner.

15. **B.** We have the results right here in our hands: Maury Povich, you ARE the answer.

QUESTIONS

16. Which trailblazing comedian got her big break with the parody song "I Made a Fool of Myself Over John Foster Dulles"?

☐ **A. Carol Burnett**
☐ **B. Phyllis Diller**
☐ **C. Joan Rivers**
☐ **D. Betty White**

---

17. *How many sisters does Joey Tribiani have on* Friends?

☐ **A. Three**
☐ **B. Five**
☐ **C. Seven**
☐ **D. Nine**

ANSWERS

16. **A.** The ode to the then–U.S. Secretary of State garnered major attention for Burnett in 1957, and she was invited to perform on *The Tonight Show* and *The Ed Sullivan Show* that year.

C. *Seven: Veronica, Mary Angela, Mary Theresa, Gina, Dina, Tina, and Cookie.* **17.**

MONEY MATTERS

1. Whose portrait was on the first one-dollar bill minted by the U.S. Treasury?

- [ ] **A. Salmon P. Chase**
- [ ] **B. George Washington**
- [ ] **C. Alexander Hamilton**
- [ ] **D. Thomas Jefferson**

2. *What is the U.S. bill with the highest monetary value?*

- [ ] **A. $500 bill**
- [ ] **B. $1,000 bill**
- [ ] **C. $10,000 bill**
- [ ] **D. $100,000 bill**

3. What is the average life expectancy for a one-dollar bill?

- [ ] **A. 6 months**
- [ ] **B. 13 months**
- [ ] **C. 21 months**
- [ ] **D. 29 months**

ANSWERS

1. **A.** The honor went to Treasury Secretary Salmon P. Chase when the first bill was issued in 1862. The more recognizable George Washington dollar began to be printed in 1869.

2. **D.** *These notes were printed in 1934 and 1935 and featured a portrait of Woodrow Wilson.*

C. Each year, 95 percent of new bills are printed to replace worn-out money. **3.**

QUESTIONS

4. How many states accept pennies at their tollbooths?

- ☐ **A. One**
- ☐ **B. Two**
- ☐ **C. Four**
- ☐ **D. Six**

The presidential profiles on the penny, the original Jefferson nickel, the dime, and the quarter all face left except for which one?

5.

- ☐ **A. Lincoln (penny)**
- ☐ **B. Jefferson (nickel)**
- ☐ **C. Franklin Roosevelt (dime)**
- ☐ **D. Washington (quarter)**

---

6. *Which of these is an example of bullion?*

- ☐ **A. Silver bar**
- ☐ **B. Beef futures**
- ☐ **C. Bonds**
- ☐ **D. Exchange traded fund**

ANSWERS

4. **A.** One. The other 49 may not have much use for the penny, but Lincoln's home state of Illinois has a soft spot for it.

5. *A. People have long imagined any number of explanations behind this about-face, but the disappointingly simple answer is that the sculptor was working from a photo in which Lincoln faced to the right.*

A. Although it shares the same root word with tasty broths (bouillon, meaning "boiling"), bullion refers to precious metals in bar or ingot form. **6.**

QUESTIONS

7. Which of these was *not* an early form of currency?

- ☐ **A. Cows and other livestock**
- ☐ **B. Salt and pepper**
- ☐ **C. Water**
- ☐ **D. Cowry shells**

8. *Since 1787, more than 300 billion pennies have been produced. About how many are currently in circulation?*

- ☐ **A. 50 billion**
- ☐ **B. 100 billion**
- ☐ **C. 150 billion**
- ☐ **D. 200 billion**

9. You have one hundred $20 bills in your hand. How many of them are likely to be counterfeit?

- ☐ **A. One**
- ☐ **B. Two**
- ☐ **C. Five**
- ☐ **D. Nine**

ANSWERS

7. **C.** Animals have long been used in trade, Roman workers were paid with salt (hence the expression "worth one's salt"), and in England in the Middle Ages, rent could be paid in peppercorns.

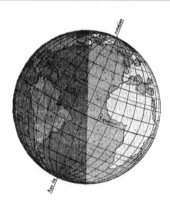

8. **C.** *That's enough pennies to circle Earth 137 times.*

9. **B.** Two. According to the U.S. Secret Service, a little less than 2 percent of American money is counterfeit, and $20 bills are popular targets, particularly for domestic counterfeiters. International counterfeiters tend to be more high rollers and prefer to mint their own $100 bills.

QUESTIONS

10. Which bill weighs the most?

- ☐ **A.** $1
- ☐ **B.** $5
- ☐ **C.** $10
- ☐ **D.** $100

---

11. *Which of these countries does* not *use the U.S. dollar as its currency?*

- ☐ **A. Zimbabwe**
- ☐ **B. Panama**
- ☐ **C. El Salvador**
- ☐ **D. Zambia**

---

12. The Chinese yuan and the Japanese yen share the same root word. What does it mean?

- ☐ **A. Paper**
- ☐ **B. Round**
- ☐ **C. Metal**
- ☐ **D. Golden**

ANSWERS

10. **Trick question.** Each bill weighs the same: one gram.

11. **D.** *Zambia uses the kwacha.*

B. The word was used to describe the shape of the coinage. **12.**

QUESTIONS

13. With an estimated net worth of $72.2 billion, Carlos Slim Helu of Mexico is one of the world's richest people. In what industry did he make his wealth?

- ☐ **A. Computers**
- ☐ **B. Finance**
- ☐ **C. Oil**
- ☐ **D. Telecommunications**

14. *Which bill is referred to as a "C-note"?*

- ☐ **A. $1**
- ☐ **B. $5**
- ☐ **C. $100**
- ☐ **D. $2**

ANSWERS

13. **D.** Slim gives new meaning to putting his money where his mouth is: He owns the telephone company Telmex, which operates the majority of Mexican landlines, as well as America Movil, the largest mobile carrier in Latin America.

C. *The $100 bill—C is the Roman numeral for 100. The bill is also sometimes called a "Benjamin," in reference to the image of Benjamin Franklin on the front.* **14.**

FAMOUS FIRSTS

1. Kokomo, Indiana, is known as the "City of Firsts." Which of these products was *not* a first for Kokomo?

☐ **A. Mechanical corn picker**
☐ **B. Stainless steel**
☐ **C. Computer**
☐ **D. Push-button car radio**

2. *Which city was the first to open a branch of the U.S. Stock Exchange?*

☐ **A. New York City**
☐ **B. Philadelphia**
☐ **C. Washington, D.C.**
☐ **D. Boston**

3. What was the first toy to be featured in a television commercial?

☐ **A. Easy-Bake Oven**
☐ **B. Barbie**
☐ **C. Mr. Potato Head**
☐ **D. Hula Hoop**

ANSWERS

1. **C.** The world's first computer was developed at the University of Pennsylvania.

In 1912, Kokomo resident Elwood Haynes developed stainless steel after his wife demanded tarnish-free dinnerware.

2. **B.** *It opened in 1790, ironically enough, at the London Coffee House.*

3. **C.** And the advertising paid off—the spud made more than $4 million in sales for Hasbro in just its first few months.

QUESTIONS

4. What was the nickname given to the first TV remote control?

- ☐ **A. Lazy Bones**
- ☐ **B. Spud**
- ☐ **C. Barcalounger**
- ☐ **D. Idle Hands**

The first pizzeria in the world opened in Naples, Italy, in 1738. What was it called? **5.**

- ☐ **A. Atza Pizzeria**
- ☐ **B. Angelo's Pizzeria**
- ☐ **C. Antica Pizzeria**
- ☐ **D. Aberto Pizzeria**

6. *What was rock music's first "supergroup"—a musical act in which all of the members had already had successful careers as part of a band or solo act?*

- ☐ **A. Cream**
- ☐ **B. Crosby, Stills & Nash**
- ☐ **C. Emerson, Lake & Palmer**
- ☐ **D. Traveling Wilburys**

ANSWERS

4. **A.** Couch potatoes everywhere rejoiced when the remote finally went public in 1956.

5. **C.** *The pizzeria features ovens lined with volcanic rock from Mount Vesuvius, and it's still in business today if you are in the neighborhood and want an "authentic" slice.*

A. Eric Clapton, Jack Bruce, and Ginger Baker were stars in their own right before they formed Cream, which released its first album in 1967. Unfortunately, the relationship soured in only two years. **6.**

QUESTIONS

7. What was the main course of the first TV dinner?

- [ ] **A. Salisbury steak**
- [ ] **B. Turkey**
- [ ] **C. Fried chicken**
- [ ] **D. Macaroni and cheese**

8. *What was the first American daily comic strip?*

- [ ] A. *The Katzenjammer Kids*
- [ ] B. *Happy Hooligan*
- [ ] C. *A. Piker Clerk*
- [ ] D. *The Yellow Kid*

9. Who was the first woman to serve on the U.S. Supreme Court?

- [ ] **A. Ruth Bader Ginsburg**
- [ ] **B. Sonia Sotomayor**
- [ ] **C. Elena Kagan**
- [ ] **D. Sandra Day O'Connor**

ANSWERS

7. **B.** Swanson had 260 tons of leftover frozen turkey after Thanksgiving in 1953, and found a clever way to turn a disaster into profit: load portions of turkey, peas, sweet potatoes, and cornbread dressing onto an aluminum tray, and voilà! A portable feast was born.

8. **C.** *The strip by Clare Briggs first appeared in the* Chicago American *in 1904.*

9. **D.** Justice O'Connor was nominated by president Reagan in 1981 and served until 2006.

One of Justice O'Connor's challenges on the High Court was finding where to go (and we don't mean "getting directions"). Since there had never been a woman on the Supreme Court before, there were no nearby women's restroom facilities.

QUESTIONS

10. Dolly, the first successfully cloned mammal, was what kind of animal?

☐ **A. Cow**
☐ **B. Pig**
☐ **C. Sheep**
☐ **D. Chicken**

11. *Elizabeth Taylor was famously married eight times. Which of these husbands was her first?*

☐ **A. Richard Burton**
☐ **B. Conrad Hilton**
☐ **C. Michael Todd**
☐ **D. Larry Fortensky**

12. Which actress was the first *Playboy* centerfold?

☐ **A. Marilyn Monroe**
☐ **B. Jayne Mansfield**
☐ **C. Bettie Page**
☐ **D. Barbara Windsor**

ANSWERS

10. **C.** Dolly the sheep lived only six years, 1996–2003. Her taxidermied remains, however, live on at the National Museum of Scotland.

11. **B.** *The hotel heir (and great-uncle to Paris and Nicky!) was married to the actress for less than a year when she was 18.*

A. Monroe didn't pose specifically for the men's magazine; publisher Hugh Hefner purchased a nude photo of the actress from another source for his inaugural 1953 issue. **12.**

QUESTIONS

13. The first nuclear explosion took place in 1945 in New Mexico. What was the name of the test project?

- ☐ A. Unity
- ☐ B. Trinity
- ☐ C. Divinity
- ☐ D. Complicity

14. *Who was the first woman in space?*

- ☐ A. Sally Ride
- ☐ B. Svetlana Savitskaya
- ☐ C. Eileen Collins
- ☐ D. Valentina Tereshkova

- ☐ A. New York City
- ☐ B. Kansas City
- ☐ C. Oklahoma City
- ☐ D. Atlantic City

15. Park-O-Meter No. 1, the world's first parking meter, was installed in 1935 at the corner of First Street and Robinson Avenue in what city?

ANSWERS

13. **B.** Trinity took place, appropriately enough, in the Jornada del Muerto (Journey of Death) desert.

D. *Tereshkova took a space ride June 16, 1963—a full 20 years before Ride became the first American woman to duplicate the feat.*

14.

15. **B.** Less than a month later, the first parking ticket was given—to a guy who swore he was just running into a store to get change for the meter. (He was a reverend, so we're inclined to believe him.)

QUESTIONS

16. The first parachutist was a brave soul who plunged 3,200 feet down to what city?

- ☐ **A. Paris**
- ☐ **B. London**
- ☐ **C. Rome**
- ☐ **D. St. Petersburg**

17. *The first credit card was introduced in New York in 1950. What was it?*

- ☐ **A. American Express**
- ☐ **B. BankAmericard**
- ☐ **C. Diners Club**
- ☐ **D. MasterCard**

18. The first moving picture copyrighted in America showed what?

- ☐ **A. An automobile racing a horse**
- ☐ **B. A lady crossing a street**
- ☐ **C. A man sneezing**
- ☐ **D. Two people kissing**

ANSWERS

16. **A.** André-Jacques Garnerin jumped from a hydrogen balloon floating above the City of Lights on October 22, 1797.

17. **C.** *Although the American Express company was established a century before Diners Club, it specialized in deliveries (as a competitor to the U.S. Postal Service), money orders, and traveler's checks. It didn't enter the credit card industry until 1958.*

C. The five-second movie, filmed by the Edison Manufacturing Company (yes, *that* Edison—he did a whole lot more than just invent the light bulb) in 1894, showed Edison's assistant Fred Ott taking a pinch of snuff and sneezing. Five stars! **18.**

QUESTIONS

19. What car make did Ray Harroun drive to victory in 1911 in the first Indianapolis 500?

- ☐ **A. Mercedes**
- ☐ **B. Marmon**
- ☐ **C. Mercer**
- ☐ **D. McFarlan**

20. *What was the first college founded in the United States?*

- ☐ **A. College of William and Mary**
- ☐ **B. Harvard University**
- ☐ **C. University of Pennsylvania**
- ☐ **D. Yale University**

ANSWERS

19. **B.** Harroun took home a whopping $14,250 prize for winning the inaugural race.

B. *Harvard was called "New College" when it was founded in 1636. Technically, Henricus Colledge was chartered first (in Virginia in 1619), but it was a casualty of the Indian uprising of 1622.* **20.**

AMERICANA

1. In which Southern state can you find the towns Republican and Democrat?

- A. North Carolina
- B. Georgia
- C. South Carolina
- D. Arkansas

2. *This'll perk you right up! Which of these is not a real town named after America's favorite caffein- ated beverage?*

- A. Hot Coffee, Mississippi
- B. Coffeeville, Alabama
- C. Coffee Creek, Montana
- D. Coffee Cup, Washington

3. Which state is home to the only active diamond mine in the United States?

- A. Montana
- B. Arkansas
- C. West Virginia
- D. Oklahoma

ANSWERS

1. **A.** Though each party is known for digging in its Tar Heels when debate season rolls around.

2. **D.** *But it's a great sponsorship opportunity for Starbucks!*

B. At Crater of Diamonds State Park, it's finders keepers (after a small entry fee, naturally). Can you dig it? **3.**

QUESTIONS

4. The United States has never lost a war in which what were used?

- ☐ **A. Torpedoes**
- ☐ **B. Horses and bayonets**
- ☐ **C. Cannons**
- ☐ **D. Mules**

How many spikes are there in the Statue of Liberty's crown? **5.**

- ☐ **A. Twelve**
- ☐ **B. Nine**
- ☐ **C. Seven**
- ☐ **D. Five**

6. *Which animal-named city is the cow-chip-throwing capital of the world?*

- ☐ **A. Buffalo, New York**
- ☐ **B. Beaver, Oklahoma**
- ☐ **C. Porcupine, South Dakota**
- ☐ **D. Alligator, Mississippi**

ANSWERS

4. **D.** Presumably the mules were just too stubborn to give up.

5. **C.** *Seven. Lady Liberty's spikes symbolize the seven seas.*

6. **B.** BYOC (Bring Your Own Chips) for this can't-miss competition each April.

QUESTIONS

7. Which woman is the subject of the most American statues?

☐ **A. Sacagawea**
☐ **B. Sojourner Truth**
☐ **C. Annie Oakley**
☐ **D. Amelia Earhart**

8. *The proud American motto "E pluribus unum"—out of many, one—was originally used by the ancient Roman poet Virgil to describe what foodstuff?*

■ **A. Lasagna**
■ **B. Salad dressing**
■ **C. Pizza**
■ **D. Dessert wine**

9. *Which of these "Alphabet Agencies" was not part of the New Deal?*

☐ **A. CCC**
☐ **B. FDIC**
☐ **C. SEC**
☐ **D. CDC**

ANSWERS

7. **A.** And if you need to settle a dispute, you can always flip a golden Sacagawea dollar.

8. **B.** *No word on whether Virgil preferred oil and vinegar over ranch.*

9. **D.** The Centers for Disease Control and Prevention (CDC) was established in 1946, about 10 years after the Great Depression and the start of the New Deal agencies. The Civilian Conservation Corps (CCC), Federal Deposit Insurance Corporation (FDIC), and Securities Exchange Commission (SEC) were part of the New Deal.

QUESTIONS

10. What was President Barack Obama's Secret Service code name?

☐ **A. Rogue**
☐ **B. Renegade**
☐ **C. Rambo**
☐ **D. Rascal**

11. *In what major city can you find the Magnificent Mile?*

☐ **A. Chicago**
☐ **B. New Orleans**
☐ **C. Seattle**
☐ **D. New York City**

12. Before it was settled in Washington, D.C., the U.S. capital was in eight other cities. Which of these did *not* serve as the capital?

☐ **A. Philadelphia, Pennsylvania**
☐ **B. Montpelier, Vermont**
☐ **C. Trenton, New Jersey**
☐ **D. Baltimore, Maryland**

ANSWERS

10. **B.** The whole Obama family had "R" code names: Michelle was Renaissance, while daughters Malia and Sasha were Radiance and Rosebud, respectively.

11. **A.** *This famous shopping destination sprawls along Michigan Avenue in the Windy City.*

12. **B.** Montpelier, Vermont, did not serve as the U.S. capital. Lancaster, Pennsylvania; York, Pennsylvania; Princeton, New Jersey; Annapolis, Maryland; and Manhattan, New York also took turns as the nation's capital.

QUESTIONS

13. Colonel Sanders (of KFC fame) was named an honorary Kentucky Colonel by the state's governor, and he's in good company. Which of these figures was *not* made an honorary Kentucky Colonel?

☐ **A. Muhammad Ali**
☐ **B. Pope John Paul II**
☐ **C. Al Gore**
☐ **D. Whoopi Goldberg**

14. *Connecticut was the first state to set a speed limit. At what "blazing" speed would cars hit that limit?*

☐ **A. 8 miles per hour**
☐ **B. 17 miles per hour**
☐ **C. 19 miles per hour**
☐ **D. 12 miles per hour**

☐ **A. Jousting**
☐ **B. Shuffleboard**
☐ **C. Dressage**
☐ **D. Sailing**

15. *Which is an official state sport of Maryland?*

ANSWERS

13. **C.** *It's hard to imagine this group sitting on the veranda drinking mint juleps together.*

14. **D.** Outside of city limits, however, cars could travel at the breakneck pace of 15 miles per hour.

15. **A.** No word on whether Medieval Times is an official restaurant, though.

QUESTIONS

16. We're used to seeing portraits of George Washington with a powdered wig. What color was his hair underneath it?

- ☐ **A. Blonde**
- ☐ **B. Brown**
- ☐ **C. Black**
- ☐ **D. Red**

17. *At which well-known vacation destination did Richard Nixon deliver his infamous "I'm not a crook" speech?*

- ☐ **A. Camp David**
- ☐ **B. Mount Rushmore**
- ☐ **C. The Grand Canyon**
- ☐ **D. Walt Disney World**

18. *Which of the following is* not *the capital of a U.S. state?*

- ☐ **A. Albany**
- ☐ **B. Carson City**
- ☐ **C. Dubuque**
- ☐ **D. Tallahassee**

ANSWERS

16. **D.** Washington was a carrottop! Thomas Jefferson and Martin Van Buren are also in the presidential redhead contingent.

17. **D.** *On November 17, 1973, Richard Nixon delivered the "I'm not a crook" speech from the Contemporary Resort inside the Walt Disney World Resort. On that day, the sprawling theme park, having opened to the public just over two years prior, may not have been the happiest place on Earth.*

C. Albany is the capital of New York, Carson City of Nevada, and Tallahassee of Florida, but Des Moines—not Dubuque—is the capital of Iowa. **18.**

GRAB BAG

1. In a period of wood and coal scarcity in nineteenth-century Egypt, what plentiful resource was used to fuel trains?

- [ ] **A. Papyrus**
- [ ] **B. Steam**
- [ ] **C. Mummies**
- [ ] **D. Lotus flowers**

2. What was the name of Olive Oyl's boyfriend before she hooked up with Popeye?

- [ ] **A. Smash Tater**
- [ ] **B. Ham Gravy**
- [ ] **C. Leafy Green**
- [ ] **D. Wing Turkey**

- [ ] **A. To Impact Personnel**
- [ ] **B. To Implement Purchase**
- [ ] **C. To Increase Performance**
- [ ] **D. To Insure Promptness**

3. *The term "tip" at restaurants was originally an acronym. What did it stand for?*

ANSWERS

1. **C.** Apparently they had "mummies to burn."

2. **B.** *Ham Gravy hired a pipe-smoking sailor to help him on a treasure hunt, and before he knew it, the sailor was putting the "Hug-ug-ug-ug-ug-ug" on his ladylove.*

3. **D.** The phrase was written on restaurant boxes, and diners put cash in the boxes before the meal to get better service.

QUESTIONS

4. What are you doing if you lacrimate?

☐ **A. Belching**
☐ **B. Sneezing**
☐ **C. Hiccupping**
☐ **D. Crying**

What curious substance did ancient Romans use as a tooth whitener? **5.**

☐ **A. Urine**
☐ **B. Clay**
☐ **C. Grass strips**
☐ **D. Crushed ants**

☐ **A. 999**
☐ **B. 119**
☐ **C. 919**
☐ **D. 199**

6. Long before the United States got 911, Great Britain developed an emergency services number. What was it?

ANSWERS

4. **D.** The technical terms for the other activities are eructation, sternutation, and singultus, respectively.

5. **A.** *Unsurprisingly, this practice petered out after a wee wee bit of time.*

6. **A.** The number was introduced in 1937, and a woman reporting a burglar outside her home made the first 999 call. The intruder was arrested, and the system was so successful that other countries started adopting it.

QUESTIONS

7. Which Pez dispenser design is the most rare?

☐ **A. Mickey Mouse**
☐ **B. Bullwinkle**
☐ **C. Daniel Boone**
☐ **D. Mr. Potato Head**

8. *Which of these animal monikers is not the name of a U.S. fraternal organization?*

☐ **A. Moose**
☐ **B. Elk**
☐ **C. Lion**
☐ **D. Cougar**

9. What is the most widely spoken language on Earth?

☐ **A. Spanish**
☐ **B. Mandarin Chinese**
☐ **C. English**
☐ **D. Russian**

ANSWERS

7. **D.** The detachable face pieces were deemed a choking hazard, and Pez pulled it from shelves after only a few months, making it a rare find indeed.

Pez made a Bullwinkle dispenser, but not a Rocky one.

8. **D.** *But we think it would be a great name for an order of women.*

B. There are about 1.1 billion native speakers of Mandarin. Even if you count all speakers of English (native speakers and those who speak it as a secondary language), it's still a distant second at 480 million. **9.**

QUESTIONS

10. In which classic game can you be ordered to "Go Directly to Jail—Do Not Pass Go, Do Not Collect $200"?

☐ **A. Risk**
☐ **B. Life**
☐ **C. Sorry**
☐ **D. Monopoly**

☐ **A. Blue**
☐ **B. Red**
☐ **C. Brown**
☐ **D. Black**

11. *What is the top-selling tie color?*

12. Which is *not* a tool used to keep time?

☐ **A. Merkhet**
☐ **B. Lathe**
☐ **C. Clepsydras**
☐ **D. Atomic clock**

ANSWERS

10. **D.** You pick your card, you take your "Chance."

The original name of the Monopoly mascot was "Rich Uncle Pennybags." Renaming him for a more politically correct era, Parker Brothers decided to go in a predictable direction: "Mr. Monopoly."

11. **A.** *No word on how many of them were purchased for Father's Day.*

B. A merkhet is an ancient Egyptian tool used to measure time by the stars, clepsydras are water clocks, and atomic clocks measure time based on how long it takes for an atom to go from negative to positive and vice versa. **12.**

QUESTIONS

13. What raucous spring celebration stems in part from the ancient Roman festivals of Saturnalia and Lupercalia?

☐ **A. April Fool's Day**
☐ **B. Easter Sunday**
☐ **C. Mardi Gras**
☐ **D. Vernal Equinox**

14. *Which planet is home to the biggest canyon in the solar system?*

☐ **A. Venus**
☐ **B. Earth**
☐ **C. Mars**
☐ **D. Jupiter**

☐ **A. Being chased**
☐ **B. Falling/flying**
☐ **C. Missing or failing an exam**
☐ **D. Death**

15. *What is the most commonly reported subject of people's dreams?*

ANSWERS

13. **C.** *In the spirit of "If you can't beat 'em, join 'em," early Christian leaders incorporated pagan rites of spring and fertility into this pre-Lenten day of gluttony.*

14. **C.** Our canyon is grand, but the Martian Mariner Valley is almost 13 times longer.

15. **A.** Being chased is by far the most-often reported theme of people's dreams. It's often interpreted as symbolic of feeling as though you are being pursued by events or unpleasant emotions in your daily life.

QUESTIONS

16. Which of the following is the traditional gift for a 25th wedding anniversary?

- ☐ **A. Diamonds**
- ☐ **B. Gold**
- ☐ **C. Platinum**
- ☐ **D. Silver**

---

17. *Benjamin Franklin is a member of 14 Halls of Fame. Which of the following is* not *one of them?*

- ☐ **A. Agricultural Hall of Fame**
- ☐ **B. American Mensa Hall of Fame**
- ☐ **C. International Swimming Hall of Fame**
- ☐ **D. World Chess Hall of Fame**

- ☐ **A. Buzz**
- ☐ **B. Chesterfield**
- ☐ **C. Fauntleroy**
- ☐ **D. Fitzgerald**

18. What is Donald Duck's middle name?

ANSWERS

16. **D.** If you're looking for something bling-ier than silver, ladies, tradition says you'll have to hang on until your 50th (gold) or 60th (diamonds) anniversary. On the "modern" gift list, diamond jewelry is recommended for the 10th anniversary, gold jewelry for the 14th, and platinum for the 20th.

17. **A.** *Among Franklin's myriad interests and talents, he was an enthusiastic and well-trained swimmer. When he was just a boy, he strapped boards to his hands in an effort to swim faster, effectively inventing the first swim paddles.*

18. **C.** "Fauntleroy" is a nice upper-class-sounding name, befitting a nephew of Scrooge McDuck, who has a fortune estimated at five billion quintiplitilion unptuplatillion multuplatillion impossibidillion fantasticatrillion dollars.

QUESTIONS

19.

Which country has the fastest trains on wheels?

☐ **A. United States**
☐ **B. France**
☐ **C. Japan**
☐ **D. Netherlands**

20.

What do meteorologists refer to when they use the term "crawler"?

☐ **A. Double rainbow**
☐ **B. Slow-moving front**
☐ **C. Tropical depression**
☐ **D. Cloud-to-cloud lightning**

21.

Approximately 20 percent of Americans have an intense, irrational fear of common things or experiences. What is the name for the fear of thunder and lightning?

☐ **A. Cacophobia**
☐ **B. Astraphobia**
☐ **C. Friggatriskaidekaphobia**
☐ **D. Trypanophobia**

ANSWERS

19.

B. The French TGV can travel as fast as 357.2 miles per hour.

On April 30, 2003, an unmanned four-stage rocket sled (a small railroad car with rockets strapped to it) reached a speed of 6,416 miles per hour at Holloman Air Force Base in New Mexico.

20.

D. One of the longest ever recorded stretched 75 miles! Makes a plain old rainbow look downright boring, doesn't it?

21.

B. The others are fear of ugliness (cacophobia), Friday the 13th (friggatriskaidekaphobia), and hypodermic needles (trypanophobia).

The fear of long words has been given a short, easy-to-remember name: hippopotomonstrosesquippedaliophobia. Try saying that one three times fast!